# Morality's Critics and Defenders

## *A Philosophical Dialogue*

# Morality's Critics and Defenders

*A Philosophical Dialogue*

Timm Triplett

Hackett Publishing Company, Inc.
Indianapolis/Cambridge

17 16 15 14      1 2 3 4 5 6 7

For further information, please address
   Hackett Publishing Company, Inc.
   P.O. Box 44937
   Indianapolis, Indiana 46244-0937

   www.hackettpublishing.com

Interior and cover designs by Elizabeth L. Wilson
Composition by Aptara, Inc.


**Library of Congress Cataloging-in-Publication Data**

Triplett, Timm, 1949–
  Morality's critics and defenders: a philosophical dialogue / Timm
Triplett.
     pages cm
  Includes bibliographical references.
  ISBN 978-1-62466-206-5 (pbk.) — ISBN 978-1-62466-207-2 (cloth)
  1. Ethics.   I. Title.
  BJ37.T75 2014
  170—dc23                                              2014011218

# Contents

*Philosophy is a shared activity, it is dialogue. And dialogue is not the simple exchange of opinions, where I have my faith, my politics and my God and you have yours. That is parallel monologue. One of the goals of dialogue is to have our opinions rationally challenged in such a way that we might change our minds. True dialogue is changing one's mind.*

~ Simon Critchley

# Preface

Nothing seems settled when it comes to opinions about what is morally right and wrong. There are fractious debates about abortion, gun control, stem cell research, the rights of animals, and limits to religious expression, to name just a few. Given the vehemence of these debates, it's unlikely that they will be resolved anytime soon.

Is there some underlying reason why this is so? When two people have a moral dispute about the correct course of action or the best social policy, they both assume that there *is* such a thing as the morally correct answer. But what if that's wrong? What if the idea that there are underlying moral truths that might resolve these debates is itself a mistake and is the reason for the lack of resolution?

If one steps away from the back-and-forth of the partisans in one particular debate to more broadly scan the global culture, the conclusion that there is no all-encompassing morality, only a diversity of voices, can seem even more compelling. Many conclude that morality must be relative to a particular cultural or ideological perspective.

But if the idea of a morality that reaches across cultures is some kind of mistake, why has it been so prominent in the history of our political, religious, and educational institutions? Maybe morality is a convenient fiction used by powerful institutions as a means of control.

Important questions such as these have led many to conclude that morality—at least as it has been traditionally conceived—is an outdated concept. But that conclusion itself is a controversial one.

This book concerns that broader debate—not the specific moral debates about contentious social policies (though some of these will be discussed) but the debate about the overall status of morality. What is morality's nature and scope? Can it survive the criticisms of moral relativists, who would deny its universal application to everyone in all societies; egoists, who would deny that it applies to themselves when they have better things to do; and fervent religious believers, who say that God's commands trump any secular moral rules when they conflict? Can Existentialist philosophers' emphasis on personal freedom and authenticity be compatible with subsuming one's life under a set of moral strictures? Is morality just a set of behaviors encoded into our genes, not the enlightened and ennobling product of reasoned reflection that some philosophers have taken it to be? Or is it, after all, simply an ideology used for social control?

The characters in this dialogue embody different critical perspectives on morality. Charlie is an atheist who looks at morality as something that limits his personal freedom. He defends the egoist idea that each of us should pursue our own goods, without obligations to anyone else. Christine thinks it impossible that the diversity of perspectives that are so prominent in the contemporary world could be compatible with the existence of a set of universal moral principles that apply to everyone. She defends the idea that morality must be understood as relative to culture, with each separate culture defining its distinctive moral views and practices. Sharifa and Matt represent, respectively, Islamic and Catholic religious perspectives. They confront the idea that morality cannot be defined in terms of religion and try to sort out how religion in general, and their religious views in particular, are distinct from and sometimes in tension with secular moral principles.

All are college students who discuss these matters with Ben, a teaching assistant in Professor Yuko Ishida's ethics course. Professor Ishida herself holds, with many philosophers starting with Thomas Hobbes, that we can learn much about morality by imagining humans in dialogue with one another. If, out of a diversity of interests, some common interests emerge in that dialogue, then we might find in what is common the basis for a common morality.

This isn't a movie or novel, so it's not a spoiler to say that the students come to be persuaded that morality can be justified, in spite of the criticisms that they consider or advocate early on in the dialogue. Although I don't endorse everything I have Professor Ishida say (sometimes I agree with Ben rather than with the professor in their conversation in the book's concluding section), I do agree with her that the deliberative structure presented here provides a useful way of supporting morality in response to the students' challenges to it (see my article noted in Further Readings for details).

But judge for yourself. I hope you will insert yourself into the dialogue and imagine what you might say in response to a point from one of the students, from Ben, or from Professor Ishida in her conversation with Ben. Might some alternative approach to one of those presented in the dialogue have produced a stronger argument, whether in support of or in opposition to the idea that morality can be justified? Does one of the arguments presented have a gap or a flaw not noticed by the other discussants? At almost any point in the dialogue, more could be said in response to a given claim. Consider how you might fill in those gaps, and think more about the views that challenge your own.

Reading philosophy is a participatory activity, even if the participants are just you and the philosopher you are reading. It's an active exchange—a dialogue—between you as a critical reader and the author. You might find your initial queries or challenges to the author's points answered in a later section, or you might not. If you read this dialogue actively, you will emerge from the encounter with a better understanding of perspectives other than your own about the nature of morality. You may well find that, like the students in this dialogue, you have by the end changed your mind.

Difficult or unusual terms are defined in the glossary in the back of the book.

For help with this book, I'm grateful to Sean McGhee, Alain Rahme, Raya Al-Hashmi, Faris Al-Hashmi, and an anonymous reviewer for Hackett. Special thanks to Chris Warden, Yutaka Yamamoto, and Donna Slonim.

I owe much of my understanding of the justification of morality to the work of Bernard Gert—work that is of great value both as a highly plausible account of morality and as a practical tool for teaching morality and for addressing specific moral dilemmas. Bernie, who died in 2011 at the age of 77 (too young!), was most generous with his time in discussing the moral system and its justification with me. This book is dedicated to his memory.

# Why Think Morality Is Universal?

*Charlie enters the philosophy student lounge and sees Christine and Sharifa studying together.*

CHARLIE: Hey guys.

CHRISTINE AND SHARIFA: Hi Charlie!

CHARLIE: I have to smile seeing you two together—from all appearances you come from different sides of the universe. The girl with the purple- and green-streaked hair and the girl with the head scarf.

CHRISTINE: Well, ever since Professor Ishida paired us up to work together on one of her philosophy problems, we've had fun working on this course together.

SHARIFA: Yes, but you know, Christine, I was kind of scared of you at first.

CHRISTINE: Scared of *me*?!

SHARIFA: Well, I just didn't know what to think. I wondered, "Is she serious? Some wild and crazy girl that I won't get along with or who will look down on me?"

CHRISTINE: But I was secretly glad when we got paired up, because I was very curious what your background was and what you were like. And I sure hope I didn't come across as looking down on you, because that's definitely not what I felt.

SHARIFA: No, you didn't come across that way at all. It didn't take long to feel comfortable with you. I'm glad now we're a team. We're very different, but it was easy right away to talk to you about the topic the professor assigned us.

CHARLIE: But didn't she assign you the question whether morality is universal? I was sure you would really disagree about that, because your backgrounds are so different.

CHRISTINE: We do disagree, but in a way that's what makes it so interesting. I felt like, well, because of our different backgrounds, her ethical and religious beliefs must be completely at odds with mine. And that's fine. I accept that, because that's just the reality. Everything's relative to a particular point of view. But then Sharifa tries to convince me that there's something universal here that the professor is talking about and that she agrees with, and I'm kind of stuck. I want to accept Sharifa's view, but in accepting it, that pushes me to challenge my own view, because the view she accepts goes against my own belief that morality is relative to a particular perspective.

SHARIFA: So it sounds like you're doing some critical thinking, just like Professor Ishida was encouraging us to do!

CHRISTINE: I guess so. But the thing I can't get around, Sharifa, is how you deal with the variety of views out there. You say morality's universal—we're all under the same moral code regarding what's right and wrong. But you believe the Islamic moral system is right, Christians believe the Christian moral system is right, and then there are people like me who don't know what to think about religion.

CHARLIE: And people like me who just don't believe in God.

CHRISTINE: Right. And then there are all the specific moral debates. Abortion, for example, which different religions have different takes on. And there are a lot of moral debates that religions don't have much to say about one way or the other.

CHARLIE: There's not much in the Bible about genetic engineering or downloading music!

SHARIFA: But remember when Professor Ishida distinguished descriptive from prescriptive statements? Descriptive statements describe how the world *is*. They claim something as a fact. Prescriptive statements say how the world *ought* to be. They include claims about what's morally right or morally wrong. Sociologists, psychologists, and pollsters can *describe* different people's beliefs, including their moral beliefs. And when they do that, they find a lot of religious and moral disagreement. But nothing about morality itself follows from the fact that there are these disagreements. Maybe one person believes abortion is morally right and another believes it's morally wrong. So far, you are just describing their different beliefs. But it may be that, in terms of prescriptive assessments, one side is really right.

CHRISTINE: Yes, but which side? You can say that your side is right, whatever side you happen to be on. But someone else will insist that they are right. So, in the end, who's to say? I mean, I respect you for holding the views you do and holding them so firmly. But I also respect the person holding the views on the other side of the debate, at least if they are sincere about it and have given it some thought, as you have. How can you say that you know your side is right?

SHARIFA: Honestly, concerning some specific moral debates, I'm not totally sure. That's one reason I took this course. I know in my heart that the way I live is a good one, and the way I've been brought up is a good one. And I know that there is evil in the world. So there has to be some account of this difference I feel between right and wrong.

CHRISTINE: How does God figure into this for you? Doesn't he provide the answers?

SHARIFA: God, or Allah, instilled in us all a sense of right and wrong. But Allah doesn't speak to us about every specific action. It's like food. Allah gave us a beautiful world that provides us with bountiful food. But he didn't tell us every little thing about what to eat and what not to eat. He gave us guidelines. We have a natural aversion to many things that would not be good for us to eat and a natural delight in many foods that are wholesome. But he didn't make us totally creatures of instinct. He does specifically forbid a few foods that we might otherwise be attracted to. But he trusts us to figure out the rest for ourselves.

It's the same with right and wrong. Allah gives us guidelines, but he also gave us our ability to reason to help us figure out how to apply those guidelines, and he gave us our hearts to care about others and feel their suffering. Here too Allah is explicit about some matters where we are particularly tempted to stray. But much has to be left up to us. Even when we know the rules, we have to decide how to apply them in specific cases. This can be hard, and we all make mistakes. But my uncertainty about the details of the morality of some specific actions doesn't mean I'm uncertain about morality as a universal order. I know that justice, kindness, and love are good, that they are universal goods for all of humanity. I know that humans make moral mistakes. They do wrong and sometimes commit serious evils. And I know that these things are wrong and evil not just in my eyes but in Allah's.

MATT [*poking his head into the room*]: Ah, I hear Sharifa fighting the good fight, defending God and universal morality. May I join you?

SHARIFA: You're more than welcome, Matt! [*To Charlie and Christine:*] Matt and I were in a comparative religion class and found ourselves defending religion together against some of the more secular students in the class.

CHARLIE: Hey, Matt. I went to that debate you were part of last semester between Christian and atheist students. I was rooting for the other side, but I had to admit you were pretty articulate.

MATT: Thanks. So did we convince you?

CHARLIE [*laughs*]: Sorry, but I guess I didn't think you were *that* articulate! But sure, join us. It balances things out with two believers and two skeptics.

I'm curious, though—you said that Sharifa was defending God when she was speaking of Allah. Isn't there a big difference there?

MATT: Not in terms of the Supreme Being we believe in. Jews, Christians, and Muslims all believe in the same God.

SHARIFA: That's right. You should take that comparative religion class, Charlie. I think even atheists would find it interesting. Allah, God, Jehovah—however you address him—it's the same Supreme Being. The stories of Abraham, Isaac, and Jacob are our stories too. The Prophet—Mohammed—sees Jesus as himself a great prophet and Jews and Christians as People of the Book.

CHRISTINE: But there have to be some differences.

SHARIFA: Of course. In Islam, we see Jesus as a great teacher but as only a human being. Even the Prophet doesn't have for us the divine status Jesus has for Christians. But the Prophet offers to humanity Allah's final revelation, completing the teachings of the earlier prophets.

MATT: Of course, that's a whole other conversation. I think you were talking about morality, not theology.

SHARIFA: Right. We were talking about whether morality is universal and objective. Christine disagrees with the position you and I would take.

CHRISTINE: And I'm still wondering how you would answer my question, Sharifa. Don't you see that someone else with completely opposite opinions about morality could feel intuitively just as certain as you that what they believe is right and that what you believe is wrong?

SHARIFA: But what do you mean "completely opposite"? I'm not sure there's anyone who goes around saying it's morally good to be mean, to kick your pets, to steal from little old ladies. I can't imagine you saying that, for example.

CHRISTINE: Of course not. But if someone did, then I wouldn't say, well, he must be wrong and Sharifa must be right. I'd say that these things are wrong according to Sharifa but right according to this other person.

MATT: Would you really accept someone who thought it was a fine thing to steal from little old ladies?

CHRISTINE: I would disagree with them because I don't believe it's right. But that's just my belief. I don't know how anyone can claim to get beyond their own personal perspective to some view that's somehow better and more objective.

SHARIFA: Is morality in your view relative to the individual? Earlier you made it sound like morality was relative to the culture.

CHRISTINE: I'm not sure at this point. Maybe it's both, or maybe that depends on the situation too?

CHARLIE: Christine, you're asking Sharifa how she can justify her moral certainty and belief in universal morality. But we can ask you in turn how you justify your idea that morality can only be defined relative to some person's or culture's beliefs and that there's nothing more objective you can say about morality. I can understand your feeling that something's troubling about the belief in some one objective moral code that applies to everybody everywhere. But isn't there something at least as troubling about "it's all relative"? That doesn't seem quite right either.

CHRISTINE: Maybe there's some middle ground, though I'm not sure what that would look like. And anyway, first you'd have to convince me that relativism is wrong, because it just seems obvious that you can't impose one moral code on everyone—and that you have to let each society and even each individual work out on their own what is moral for them.

MATT: Listen, I have to go. But this is all pretty interesting, and I'm curious about the variety of perspectives the four of us bring to this topic. Do you think we could all meet once a week to discuss this more? I could make myself available at this time.

CHARLIE: Sure. I'm free.

SHARIFA: It would be a great way to think more about what we're learning in Professor Ishida's class.

CHRISTINE: Great idea—see you all next week!

# Problems with Moral Relativism

*One week later.*

CHRISTINE: I know Professor Ishida believes that morality is universal. But with all due respect—and I do respect her—it just seems arrogant to me to think that there's one morality that applies to everyone. Last week, Charlie asked how I can defend the idea that morality is relative, so I've given that some thought. I guess I just start with the fact that there have been so many cultures in history with so many different views about morality. We celebrate the ancient Greeks, but they were fine with having slaves.

MATT: So what are you saying morality is then?

CHRISTINE: I think you can only talk about morality relative to a specific culture and its moral codes. Something's moral if it's accepted in a culture. You can't come from outside that culture and criticize that culture's practices.

MATT: It seems to me that that can't be right. As a Christian, I believe in God's universal morality. But, independently of my religious beliefs, I think there are arguments against your cultural relativism about morality.

You say that we celebrate the Greeks, and that they had slaves. But maybe *that's* not what we celebrate them for. They had great art and architecture, playwrights, philosophers. They were full of new ideas. But they didn't change everything at once. We don't admire them because they had slaves. They weren't different from other ancient societies in that way. We admire them for what they did and thought that was new.

CHRISTINE: But *why* did everyone have slaves then? Your attitude seems to be that slavery was wrong in ancient Greece, even if that society did do some admirable things. But I'm not sure slavery was wrong for them. They had to rely on manual labor for everything. No electricity, no dishwashers, no pickup trucks. It's easy for us to look down on them. But if we're going to evaluate them, we have to look at things from their perspective. What alternative could they have had, especially if some in their culture were to have the luxury to begin to develop Western civilization?

SHARIFA: Professor Ishida made the point that "ought" implies "can." As I understood that, she meant that if a person *ought* to do something, it has to be true that they are actually *able* to do it. It's unfair to morally criticize someone who had no choice or ability to act. So, say a building collapses during an earthquake and a bystander sees someone become trapped underneath falling debris. He runs over and does everything he can to lift the debris the victim is trapped under, but it's just too heavy. The person unfortunately dies. No one would criticize the bystander. If anyone said, "You ought to have saved that person's life!" that would be unfair, because they just didn't have the physical strength to free the person.

CHRISTINE: I remember that point. But I don't see what it has to do with the Greeks.

SHARIFA: Well, you supposed that the Greeks had no alternative but to have slaves. If that were true, then they couldn't be blamed for having them, just like we couldn't blame the person for failing to rescue the earthquake victim.

CHRISTINE: So that would make my point that slavery is morally acceptable in that society.

SHARIFA: Not really. Suppose we accept that the ancient Greeks had no choice but to have slaves in order for their economy to be sustained and their city-states to survive. This wouldn't be an endorsement of slavery, not even a relativistic endorsement, any more than the earthquake case is an endorsement of letting people die. If you *could* have helped that person trapped under the debris, then you should have done so. In the same way, maybe slavery is morally bad in itself, and any time a society can avoid it, it should, even if it can't be criticized in those circumstances, if there are any, in which it has no other choice. So maybe the Greeks can't be morally criticized, not because slavery is morally right for them, or for anyone, but because they had no economic choice.

CHARLIE: But I'm not sure they really had no control over that.

SHARIFA: I'm not either. My point is just that *if* slavery was economically necessary at some stage or stages of human history and there was no feasible economic alternative, then our inability to criticize those societies morally for slavery doesn't support moral relativism. It just supports the "ought implies can" point. Or really the other side of that coin—if "ought implies can," then "can't" implies that it would be unfair to impose a moral evaluation on the situation, person, or society in question.

MATT: And to the extent that a society *could* avoid slavery—which after all is the use of a person as property, working for no pay, under the complete control of the owner who can separate husband from wife or mother from child if he wants to—then it seems reasonable to think that a society ought to use those other non-slaveholding options and not treat people in that way.

CHRISTINE: But I think there are clearer cases that do support moral relativism. There are just so many disagreements where it seems like individuals and societies *do* have choices. In modern societies, there are some that have capital punishment, while others reject it. It seems clear that a contemporary society has the freedom to choose either option and so is morally responsible for its choice. It's always a choice for a woman whether to have an abortion and for a society what laws to set regarding abortion. And yet different religions, governments, and individuals disagree about the moral acceptability of abortion.

We can only understand things from our own point of view, and sometimes that's a very limited perspective. How can we pronounce on the sexual morality of cultures that see things very differently? Think of how Victorians would look at the idea of gay people marrying! It's not that they're wrong and we're right. It's just that it's all so different. Marriage of gay people is just not something that was even on their radar.

CHARLIE: Maybe that was just a matter of ignorance or lack of options in those days.

CHRISTINE: Well, maybe from our perspective we fail to see options that other cultures see.

One of my classmates in high school was born in India. She was betrothed to a boy when they were both just young children. I thought at first that this was a terrible constriction of her freedom. But she herself was very happy and excited about it—about going back to India to marry him when she graduated from high school, instead of staying here and going to college. She had an interesting perspective on our culture that made me think twice about a lot of our cultural assumptions. She said that in America everything is based on individualism and individual choice, whereas in India such important choices are a family matter. She felt that that was better—that she has a better chance of having a good marriage when it's based on the collective wisdom and strong support of two good families, instead of when it's based on a decision of two young people by themselves who can't really have the most mature perspectives on life yet.

CHARLIE: But would you want *your* family to make that choice for you, rather than you yourself?

CHRISTINE: No. But that's my culture. If I had been raised in an Indian family, maybe I would be happy with those arrangements and critical of the American you're-on-your-own style of doing things. I'm not saying one is right and the other is wrong. I'm saying you can't make some ultimate moral judgment that one is better than the other.

CHARLIE: But here you are in college, independent, learning a lot, having lots of potential for your future life. Instead of going to college, your high school friend will be somebody's wife in a culture that doesn't offer as many opportunities for women.

CHRISTINE: I'm glad I'm pursuing the life I am but so is my friend in pursuing her life. Good luck to both of us in our different ways of pursuing happiness! As for opportunities for women, my friend did suggest that women weren't as independent in most parts of Indian society as in ours. But we're arrogant to think that equality has to be defined just the way we define it. In India, they have an equality, a balance. It's just equal in a different way.

CHARLIE: Hmm. That kind of reminds me of George Orwell's *Animal Farm*. "All animals are equal but some animals are more equal than others." I think it's dangerous to talk about different kinds of equality. It risks having one group treated less fairly than another.

SHARIFA: I can understand your point, Christine, that women in India can be happy under a different system, and a different kind of equality, than in the U.S. I feel that way myself, growing up with a set of values from my family and my mosque that are different in a lot of ways from what's common in the U.S., and I think better. I think women and men *are* different and that you do have to think in terms of different expectations and rules. But it can go too far. Different doesn't have to mean superior/inferior. So to that extent I agree with you and disagree with Charlie. But I agree with Charlie that there are limits to judging each culture's different attitudes as morally on a par. Some aspects of traditional Hindu and, I'm sorry to say, Muslim cultures go too far in their ways of treating women very differently from men. So in places like Afghanistan and Africa, as well as India and Pakistan, there are terrible abuses of power. The idea that girls should not get an education, that it's the woman's fault if she's raped, that a practice like bride burning is socially accepted—you just can't go that far. All women have a basic right to an education, and no woman wants to be killed because her family isn't wealthy enough to suit some other family. Even in Egypt—we've gone back sometimes to visit relatives—I don't like the inequality there—the way women are treated.

CHRISTINE: Is it really literally bride burning?

SHARIFA: Yes! Women can be killed—and sometimes still are in India today—if the family of the groom doesn't feel that her dowry is high enough. Or sometimes just to eliminate her so the husband or his family can acquire another dowry. There are hundreds of cases of such killings in India every year.

I can easily believe that your Indian high school friend is happy— just as I am happy in my life that recognizes real differences in roles for women and men. But there are many women in these cultures who are deeply unhappy. There has been an epidemic of women in Afghanistan dousing themselves with kerosene and setting themselves on fire. They are miserable because they are married off to abusive husbands, and they have no recourse.

CHRISTINE: That's horrible. But abusive men and mistreated women are unfortunately not confined to these cultures. It happens all too often here.

CHARLIE: Yes, but here women have social and legal support.

SHARIFA: Right. In India and Afghanistan, for example, the legal system often isn't in place to protect these women or challenge these backward attitudes and practices. Or even if it is in place, it's sometimes not really enforced, especially in more rural areas.

And anyway, isn't it objectively wrong when a husband abuses his wife physically or emotionally? It doesn't matter what culture it happens in or whether the practice is generally accepted there. It's just wrong. And to me that shows that morality can't be reduced to what a culture holds to be right or wrong.

CHRISTINE: I can't really disagree with that. It does look like *some* things—and I emphasize the "some"—are objectively wrong, and not just wrong according to a particular culture. And you haven't even brought up the example often used of the Holocaust. So yes— there can be objectively wrong practices even if the culture, or the powerful elements within it, support that practice.

But you can't just leave things there. I think this idea of objective or universal morality can make people arrogant. It leads them to think that true morality is whatever their religion or culture says it is, and that everyone else is wrong. They judge other cultures without even trying to understand them. And that itself is wrong.

# Exploring Morality across Cultures

SHARIFA: Christine, you missed Professor Ishida's lecture last week. What happened?

CHRISTINE: I'm sorry I missed it. I was sick.

SHARIFA: I'm glad you're better now. But it's too bad you missed it. I thought it was quite relevant to our last discussion.

CHRISTINE: So tell me about it!

SHARIFA: You were saying that we had to respect that other cultures just saw things differently, and so we couldn't judge them morally. But Professor Ishida talked about her experience as a Japanese American. She thought it was amusing that non–Japanese Americans would often talk about how inscrutable the Japanese were. She gave the example of how President Nixon was visiting Japan and couldn't understand the Japanese prime minister. This example has been used by some Westerners to argue that there are these impenetrable barriers to understanding the Japanese, including their sense of right and wrong. Here's a passage from the reading she gave us [Reads:] "President Nixon asked for a cut in Japanese textile exports, and Prime Minister Sato answered, 'Zensho shimasu,' which was translated literally as 'I'll handle it as well as I can.' Nixon thought that meant 'I'll take care of it,' but the Japanese understood it to mean something like 'Let's talk about something else.'"

Apparently Nixon was outraged and thought Prime Minister Sato had deceived him. But the prime minister was just speaking indirectly in the Japanese manner. He may have felt that President Nixon would have lost face by having his request rejected. Far from wanting to deceive anyone, the prime minister may have just been trying, in the Japanese way, to protect the president from embarrassment and loss of status.

CHRISTINE: Right. So that's like what I was getting at last week about how we unfairly judge other cultures without understanding them. What you read is a good example of where we rushed in and decided that somebody in another culture acted immorally, and it wasn't really immoral at all. We can't presume to understand these other cultures; but we judge them anyway.

SHARIFA: Someone asked Professor Ishida how this was supposed to go against moral relativism, since it looked like she was saying that Japanese morality really was different from Western morality. She said that her main point for now was that Japanese morality was not inscrutable—not something Westerners were simply incapable of understanding. She said that a person like herself would be impossible if that were so. She's Japanese American and grew up in California. She says that her parents were fairly traditional and kept to traditional Japanese and Buddhist values. But she also went to public elementary school and got the whole dose of American culture and feels completely American. She said that, just as there are bilingual people who understand two or more languages very well, she was sort of ethically bilingual.

CHRISTINE: You know, it sounds kind of like you, just with a different country in the background.

SHARIFA: That's right! I loved hearing her talk about this because there's a lot in what she described about growing up in two cultures that I've experienced too, except that where her background is Japanese and Buddhist, mine is Egyptian and Islamic, but both of us feel completely American, having grown up here.

Anyway, she said that she doesn't think the differences between Japanese and American values amount to relativism. She thinks that there's some kind of universal morality embracing all cultures and that, while there are some differences among cultures in what they emphasize, such differences can all fall within this overarching moral system. She said that any reasonable concept of morality has to allow for some variation in behavior, where behavior not considered appropriate in one culture might be morally acceptable in the other. And because of that variation, sometimes one culture can have a hard time understanding another.

CHRISTINE: Just like with people!

SHARIFA: That's right. A more outgoing individual can have a hard time understanding someone who's more shy and vice versa. But these can just be differences of preference and emphasis, not differences regarding what's morally right and morally wrong. In principle, Professor Ishida says, understanding these differences in this way is always possible. Just as an outgoing person who really cares about and spends time with an introvert can come to understand why they behave the way they do and what's motivating them and a shy person can likewise come to understand an extroverted person, so those from one culture can come to understand the actions and motivations of those in another that may initially appear puzzling. This understanding isn't automatic but can happen if they become familiar enough with that culture and approach it with an open-minded attitude.

CHRISTINE: But how does this actually work in comparing Japanese and Western morality? Maybe you have to be "bi-ethical" like Professor Ishida herself to really understand these things.

SHARIFA: Professor Ishida thinks that the Japanese conception of morality can come to be understood by anyone from another culture who approaches it in a sympathetic spirit and spends some time getting to know the culture. For example, the prime minister's action with President Nixon was an example of the practice of something called [*looking at her class notes*] "*haragei.*" It's a kind of indirectness in speech, seen as a virtue insofar as it's intended to prevent offense to another person or to not appear too presumptuous or aggressive. Supposedly, another Japanese person will understand that someone she is talking to is practicing *haragei* when this is so and understand the implications of it. If Prime Minister Sato had been talking to another Japanese individual, he or she would presumably have understood that the prime minister was not agreeing to cut textile imports. So there's no deep mystery about what *haragei* is or how it can be used. This isn't to say that it can't be misunderstood, or misused. Professor Ishida said that the Japanese themselves often complain about it. But if one is familiar with the practice and is looking for it, it can in many cases be easy enough to spot and understand.

She also said that this kind of practice may exist to such a degree in a culture like Japan because it's a quite homogeneous culture. Maybe conversation in American culture is more candid and blunt because it has to be that way, given the diversity of cultures that make it up. That makes it hard for something pretty subtle like "saying X by saying Y" to be a common understanding that is part of the broader culture. Even within American culture, though, this kind of implicit understanding can occur within subcultures or among individuals very familiar with each other.

CHRISTINE: I think I see what you mean about subcultures. When it comes to things like fashion or ways of talking, there can be a subculture within a society that defines what's cool or socially acceptable. Maybe something just a bit different feels uncool or off to those in that subculture, but it can be a subtle thing, where those not in the loop are mystified about how those standards apply. But there's really something to the difference. You just have to be attuned to it to see it.

But how do you get one universal system of morality out of these differences that make it so easy for Americans to misunderstand Japanese and vice versa?

SHARIFA: Professor Ishida said she will discuss that in more detail when she outlines the general features of the moral system as a whole. But one point she made toward that, using this example about conversations, was that American and Japanese conversational values, while very different, can both aim toward an overarching universal moral value. These conversational values are just different cultures' ways of differently practicing universal values that both cultures hold in common, like not harming another person either physically *or* emotionally. And that's the key for Professor Ishida: the different Japanese and American conversational values are just different specific ways of applying the *universal* value of not hurting or offending others. And this could be so even though a conversational practice that might be morally acceptable in America might be morally wrong in Japan, because there, but not in America, it would be taken as too blunt, insulting, and offensive.

CHRISTINE: It's pretty interesting stuff. I'm sorry I missed the class. I'll have to think about it.

MATT: Another thing to think about, Christine, is that your own criticisms about the way we can be so arrogant and culturally insensitive are themselves actually moral judgments that cross cultural lines. If Nixon was unfair in his moral judgment of Sato as deceitful, then where is that judgment of unfairness coming from, if all values are culturally determined? Maybe Nixon's attitude is just right according to his culture. You're very concerned about cultural arrogance—particularly our culture unfairly judging other cultures or imposing its views on others. But if you say that's morally wrong, then aren't you saying that one culture's intolerance of another is a morally bad thing?

CHRISTINE: American intolerance of other cultures is bad.

MATT: But you'd have to say any culture's intolerance of any other culture is bad, yes?

CHRISTINE: I guess so. Sure.

MATT: So tolerance is a universal value that isn't dependent on what any one culture thinks. If one culture tries to lord it over other cultures or justifies wars or other destructive actions on the grounds of its alleged cultural superiority, we can say that that's wrong only if there is some kind of morality that transcends that particular culture's judgment of its own superiority.

CHRISTINE: OK. You guys are giving me a lot to think about! I already agree that there are some actions that are just objectively wrong, even if a culture approves of it. I guess in some ways you are making that same point from another perspective: that if American culture tends to be insensitive to or intolerant of Japanese culture because Americans have different values, then the moral relativists would have to say that those American values are right according to American culture, wrong according to Japanese culture, and that's all you can say. But I agree that that doesn't seem right. Actually I can say something stronger than that: The American intolerance or negative judgment of the Japanese is objectively wrong or at least (if it's a misunderstanding, as with President Nixon thinking the Japanese prime minister was deceitful) unfair and insensitive.

MATT: But also that a similar intolerance toward the Americans on the part of the Japanese is also morally unfair. Meaning, everyone's equal in this regard precisely *because* values like tolerance are universal. I understand your criticisms of the impact of American political policies and cultural practices on the rest of the world. It can be and has been arrogant and elitist. But America is not historically unique in that respect. Leading up to the Second World War, the Japanese were pretty full of themselves as the superior culture, and during the war they were pretty horrible to the Koreans and Chinese, beyond what might be justified in wartime. It's just objectively true that intolerance is wrong, no matter which culture might practice it. In fact two cultures could both be wrong if they were intolerant toward each other.

CHRISTINE: Well, *that's* a happy thought. But I can't really disagree with anything you're saying here. I guess the thing that still bothers me is—I don't see that *every* action has an objectively correct right or wrong answer regarding its morality. It's one thing to say, at the level of criticizing other cultures, that the Holocaust was objectively morally wrong or, at the level of criticizing other individuals, that a con artist scamming people out of all their money is objectively morally wrong. But it still seems to me as though the morality of many or most actions doesn't have an objectively right or wrong answer. At the cultural level, how can there be some one right answer about abortion or capital punishment or gun control or gay marriage?

And at the personal level, my boyfriend says his boss is asking him to cut corners to make cheaper print cartridge refills. He's selling a lot of cartridges that he knows aren't going to last very long. He wonders whether he should leave his job, call his boss out, or just let things be. It's not like it's a life-or-death matter. No one will die because of a poor quality ink-jet cartridge. But it still bothers him. And when I listen to him discuss all the ins and outs and complications and options about what he should do, I have to wonder: How is there some one morally correct answer to a problem like that?

SHARIFA: Professor Ishida, responding to the question about relativism from a student in class last week, mentioned that she didn't think *every* moral question had a single right or wrong answer.

CHRISTINE: But then how is that compatible with moral objectivism?

SHARIFA: I'm not sure. I think it has something to do with there being two separate questions. First, is morality objective in the sense that there exist objective moral truths that are not determined by a culture but are true or false in spite of what a culture might believe about the morality of the action in question? And second, is it true that for every possible action an individual person could undertake, and for every cultural practice, there is one and only one correct answer as to whether that action is morally right or morally wrong? I think she wants to say that you aren't contradicting yourself if you believe that there's a positive answer to the first question and a negative one to the second. I guess we'll find out more about what she thinks. It's still early in the semester.

CHRISTINE: This possibility is really interesting to me. I had always thought that if you're an objectivist about morality, you have to believe that every action is either morally right or morally wrong. The approach you're describing may really be what I was looking for concerning morality. I never wanted to suggest that genocide was morally right.

But how does Professor Ishida distinguish between cases where there is a definite moral answer and cases where there's not?

SHARIFA: I'm not sure about that either. She said she would be talking about it.

# Why Should I Be Moral?

CHRISTINE: Charlie, where are you coming down here? You've been critical of relativism. Does that mean you accept universal morality?

CHARLIE: Well, what does universal morality amount to? I'm still not sure.

SHARIFA: Professor Ishida said she would go into the details later. But basically she said it could be thought of as a set of principles concerning how we treat each other, where these principles have the goals of encouraging ways in which we benefit each other and minimizing ways in which we cause each other harm. It's universal because it applies equally to everyone. It includes a system of rewards and punishments based on how well a particular behavior conforms to these goals of helping and not hurting others.

CHARLIE: Something like that sounds way too intrusive. I didn't come into the world for the sake of other people. Of course, fair is fair; they didn't come into the world for my sake either. What morality does is limit me and restrict my freedom and other people's as well. With all due respect to Sharifa and Matt, I think we've had too much of religions telling us what to do and how to behave. And I'm not criticizing them because they are *religions*. The whole idea of limitations imposed on us by some universal morality is something we need to get free of. Especially this idea of benefiting others. I shouldn't be required to help the other guy. In fact, I think that that can keep the other guy from being self-reliant. It shouldn't be up to some external authority, whether it's a religion, a government, or some abstract set of rules, to tell me how to live my life.

And all this talk of morality and moral ideals—compare it with how people actually behave. Sometimes the people who profess morality to the skies are the worst offenders—and here I *am* thinking of religion in particular. So the Catholic Church has all these restrictive teachings, like "no sex before marriage; birth control is wrong." But then some priest sexually abuses children, and his superiors cover it up. I mean, a priest is supposed to be celibate, and here some of them are not just having sex but sexually abusing little kids. Such incredible hypocrisy!

MATT: But Charlie, you know that Church teaching is totally against such sexual abuse. That's not Catholicism. That's individuals going astray.

CHARLIE: Sometimes they're individuals in pretty powerful positions.

MATT: Granted, and the more powerful they are, the more horrible it is, because it means the abuse can spread when they pretend not to see what's going on and shift an abusive priest to another diocese. I'm totally with you on the hypocrisy and the horror of the abuse. But it's an argument against individuals and some parts of the institution, not against the morality preached by the Church. Sure, there are always hypocrites. But you can't use that kind of behavior to undermine the moral facts themselves.

CHARLIE: What good are any "moral facts" if no one follows them?

CHRISTINE: I've often wondered about that. Maybe everyone really is just in it for themselves.

CHARLIE: And what's so wrong about that? Look, if I see a chance to cheat on a biology exam in a class I need for pre-med, who gets hurt if I do cheat? I'm not saying I did or will. But maybe I need that grade to continue in the program. And if my goal is to become a doctor, that's a good thing. Good for me, good for society.

MATT: Well, you don't take tests in a vacuum. Cheating does hurt other students. You get a better ranking than you deserve, and that means students who are actually better candidates can lose out in terms of class rankings, financial aid opportunities, and letters of recommendation.

SHARIFA: I'm not sure I'd want to have a doctor who got where he did by cheating in med school.

MATT: And even if you did end up being a good doctor and helping your patients, notice that the justification you offered depends on the claim that you are doing good for other people. So you're really not thinking just in terms of yourself and your own interests after all.

CHARLIE: Well, I don't mind if something that I do because it's in my interests helps others, as long it's like a doctor helping a patient, where it gives the person helped freedom from illness instead of making them more dependent, and as long as those I help don't come to think of it as some sort of obligation I have to them. It's a trade relationship—the doctor gets paid a fair price in exchange for his medical expertise and help. It's not a moral requirement on my part to aid others, and I don't do it for that reason.

SHARIFA: Charlie, I have to take issue with your suggestion that no one follows the rules of morality except when it's compatible with their own self-interests. You may act only with yourself in mind, but a lot of people take a sense of morality and responsibility to others seriously. We do think we have obligations to others. My religion tells me this, but my own sense of connection with others tells me this too.

CHARLIE: Fine, but what if *I* don't have that sense of connection? If *you* have it, then you're helping others because that's what makes you feel good. I think it's just a fact that everyone acts in terms of their own self-interests.

SHARIFA: So you have some special insight into my and everyone else's motivations?

CHARLIE: Well, why would you do it if it didn't make you feel good?

SHARIFA: I suppose that if I said it's because sometimes I care more about helping someone else, even if it is difficult for me or even if it puts me at a disadvantage, you'd say that I would not do something like that unless I wanted to do it, all things considered, and that if I want to then it's still about me and my wants. You can always make that claim, I guess. But, putting myself out of the picture, I think that saying everyone acts from selfish motives does a real injustice to a lot of people. It's putting everyone in the same pigeonhole—maintaining that everyone is equally selfish. I just don't think everyone is the same in that respect. Some people are considerate; some aren't. Some think a lot about other people and their needs; others think almost entirely about themselves. Some are motivated out of sympathy and compassion to lend a hand to others. Some can't be bothered.

I think it's unfair to those who act compassionately to put them in the same self-regarding category as the manipulative jerk. These are real differences in people, and they make a moral difference. I know which kind of person I would rather be around and hope to become myself.

MATT: I wonder if some people like to say everyone is selfish because it's just a way of justifying and rationalizing their own selfish behavior. "Everyone does it, so it's OK for me to do it."

CHARLIE: Well, I don't say that everyone does it. At least, maybe everyone is selfish at bottom, but they're not all selfish in the right way. I think that when you act on behalf of others, you make them helpless or keep them helpless. So I'd say compassion and altruism are really as selfish as the actions of a person who focuses just on himself, but it's the wrong kind of selfishness.

MATT: But once again here, you're actually trying to justify selfish behavior by saying it benefits everyone. So you're not really accepting selfishness as an end or value in and of itself. You just disagree on what the best way to achieve those societal benefits is.

CHRISTINE: And I want to know, Charlie, what you think about Sharifa's point that it seems unfair to lump everyone together as equally selfish. Even if you think compassionate people are wrong to be that way, aren't there real differences in character between them and someone who only thinks about himself and doesn't care about others? And would you really rather surround yourself with people like that?

CHARLIE: I'll admit that these kinds of differences in people's psychology and character do exist. But I question putting the moral value on the side of the "compassionate" person, rather than the one who operates from self-interest. If another person who values self-interest is honest in their dealings with me, I think I would rather have them as my friend and associate instead of someone who acts out of misguided compassion. I don't want or need their support. I'm best off if I support myself.

SHARIFA: Supposing that you are *able* to support yourself.

MATT: And Charlie, notice how you invoke honesty. But it isn't always in a person's self-interest to be honest. So you are drawing on something that has to do with a traditional moral value— being honest—that's independent of self-interest. It sounds like you wouldn't want to have business dealings or be in a relationship with someone who out of self-interest didn't deal honestly with you but was a manipulative liar.

CHARLIE: That's true. Look, I understand that you have some good points here. And I'm a big believer in reason. So I want to think about the reasons pro and con. But by the same token, you have to openly consider my arguments for my position. I don't think anything we've said here proves anything one way or the other.

SHARIFA: Well, Professor Ishida's view is that her hypothetical deliberative committee explains how morality can be justified in preference to the sorts of attitudes and philosophies that emphasize self-interested approaches.

CHRISTINE: But I still don't get what this deliberative committee is and how it's supposed to work.

CHARLIE: It does sound pretty interesting. If there's some reasonable argument here against my position, I really want to see it. But I don't think I understand it either.
You know who this means we have to talk to?

CHRISTINE AND SHARIFA: Ben!

CHARLIE: Everybody's favorite TA!

# The Deliberative Committee

CHRISTINE: Ben, thanks for meeting with us. We really appreciate your taking the time.

BEN: I'm happy to. I love getting urgent emails from students who need to talk philosophy! You have questions about the deliberative committee?

CHARLIE: Yes, we've been talking about this hypothetical deliberative committee that Professor Ishida said was her organizing concept for thinking about morality and about the ways in which the idea of some kind of universal morality has been criticized. We still don't understand what the committee is supposed to do or how it works. Can you explain that for us?

BEN: Sure. Professor Ishida imagines a deliberative committee consisting of ordinary people—drawn from all walks of life and belonging to different cultures and ethnicities. The more diversity the better, since Professor Ishida wants to see what the results of the deliberations look like no matter who might be put on the committee. This committee is given the task of determining the kind of society that the members of the committee and everyone else will subsequently live in. It's a thought experiment, of course. No one is actually in a position to determine social organization at this level. But suppose it were so and that what this deliberative committee decided actually did become the set of rules regulating their and everyone else's lives going forward. Their decision would be issued as a public endorsement of some system of principles or rules for governing social interactions. The rules would determine which kinds of behaviors are to be promoted and rewarded, which are to be discouraged and punished. The deliberative committee would not have the job of deciding specific rewards and punishments for each kind of behavior—a near endless task. It would decide broadly among different and competing general systems for determining rewards and punishments.

Professor Ishida's idea is that this is a way of responding to the critics of morality. She claims that her hypothetical scenario justifies morality by showing that the moral system is to be preferred to any non-moral system proposed by its critics.

MATT: So what's the moral system, and who are its critics?

BEN: The moral system as Professor Ishida envisions it is a universal and objective system concerning human interactions and how society regulates them. The governing principles of the moral system have the aim of promoting actions that are helpful to others and discouraging actions that are harmful. Such principles would encourage acts of charity or kindness, for example, and discourage actions that cause pain, deprive others of freedom, or otherwise cause harm or increase the risk of causing harm. The system also includes guidelines for meting out praise and blame, rewards and punishments, in accordance with how well or badly individuals comply with the other principles. A supporter of the moral system, emphasizing what humans have in common, believes that these basic principles apply to all humans—they are universal.

CHRISTINE: There's just one moral system?

BEN: Talk of *the* moral system is actually a bit misleading, since there are competing theories of morality that all qualify as advocating these broad aims. Later I'll say more about the specific features that all moral systems have in common and that differentiate them from non-moral systems.

CHARLIE: What do the critics of morality say?

BEN: Critics of this basic idea can object to the moral system's universality and objectivity, to its preeminence over other systems, or to the need for or desirability of having *any* overarching system, moral or otherwise.

One critical take is the idea that morality is culturally relative. This view rejects the universality claimed by the proponent of the moral system. Where the moral system emphasizes commonalities among all humans, cultural relativism emphasizes how humans are differently shaped by their cultures. The relativist will argue that it's the culture that should determine how various behaviors of its members are to be rewarded, permitted, and punished. So if the deliberative committee were to choose the cultural relativist system, it would be allowing each culture or society to determine its own rules.

Religious systems focus on rewarding, allowing, and punishing behavior according to whether an action is thought by adherents to be pleasing to God as they conceive God, or is otherwise in accordance with tenets outlined in teachings and writings they take to be foundational to their religion. The idea of a religious system as an alternative to the moral system is that if a religious system is adopted by the deliberative committee, its rules, principles, and doctrines override those of the moral system when there is a conflict. In many or most cases, religious teachings are perfectly compatible with morality. But in other cases, a religion might make obligatory an action that morality would merely permit, like a commandment to pray or to attend or support a church. Sometimes, in the name of God or their religion, religious institutions and their leaders advocate actions in opposition to the moral system, such as orders or requirements to condemn, deprive of freedom, or even kill those who don't worship in accord with the dictates of their religion. When religion goes in that direction, as Christianity did for example during the Spanish Inquisition, it becomes an enemy of morality, even if it claims that the teachings are justified as God's commands.

These are just a couple of the alternative systems for regulating behavior that the deliberative committee would consider. But Professor Ishida thinks that the deliberative committee ultimately will choose the moral system over all the alternatives.

CHRISTINE: I have a question about this whole idea of social systems that regulate behavior and dole out rewards and punishments. The deliberative committee decides on a particular system, and that system then becomes the one under which the members of the committee and everyone else live from that point on. But I'm not sure what that means. What would it be to live under the moral system, for example? Would there be a bunch of Morals Police roaming the streets telling people what to do? And since people can treat others immorally in the privacy of their homes—I'm thinking of everything from treating a spouse or child rudely, to cheating in a relationship, to murder—would there be enforcers snooping in people's houses or shining flashlights through the windows?

SHARIFA: Well, in the case of something as serious as murder, you *do* want the police to come in and investigate and use the justice system to punish the perpetrator.

CHRISTINE: I guess so. But I sure don't want Morals Cops hanging around checking to make sure no one is being rude or following me around to see whether I'm cheating on my boyfriend.

BEN: I suppose one of the systems to be considered could be the one you're imagining, where spies or police are everywhere checking on people. There are even historical and contemporary examples of such societies. But those kinds of societies have typically been concerned with the enforcement of the reigning political or religious ideology, even though morality is sometimes used as a cover. I doubt that our deliberative committee would endorse such a society. But that remains for you as deliberators to examine for yourselves.

CHRISTINE: So *we're* on the committee?

BEN: Yes. The way Professor Ishida has set up her thought experiment, each person can imagine being on the committee, bringing his or her existing beliefs and perspectives to the deliberative table, and interacting with others who will have their often very different beliefs and perspectives. She really does have in mind ordinary people, not unrealistic idealizations.

CHRISTINE: But if endorsing the moral system isn't choosing to live in a police state, then what is it?

BEN: There can be a lot of different kinds of societies that could be said to follow the moral system, just as there are a lot of different kinds of societies that could be called democracies. But the idea of morality embraces even more variety than the idea of democracy, because democracy is concerned with the formal, political structure of a society, while morality is an informal system. That means it's not something set up by a constitution or the judicial system. Morality is much broader than that. As some of Christine's examples suggest, it includes concern with everyday interpersonal behavior, a lot of which no one thinks should be *formally* rewarded or punished, for example

with prison terms or fines. One person can be really mean to someone else or manipulative toward his friends or partner or whomever.
And that's a moral issue—the mean or manipulative person is a jerk.
He's morally wrong to treat others in the way he does. But if this
meanness doesn't rise to a sufficiently high level of emotional abuse
or physical harm, which very often it doesn't, it's not the sort of thing
we think the formal structures of control in society should come in
and deal with. Somebody may be a jerk, but that doesn't mean we
think he should be taken away by the police and put in jail.

But it also doesn't mean there's no recourse. As an informal system,
the moral system includes a lot of informal rewards and punishments.
So one way to punish the jerk is to avoid him. Maybe when he real-
izes he has no friends, he starts getting the idea. Or we can talk to him
about how hurtful his behavior is.

CHRISTINE: I'm not sure talking to a jerk ever does any good.
They're too full of themselves.

BEN: I'm sure that's true in a lot of cases. But you don't want to
make that assumption about every such case. Sometimes a person
behaving in a rude or obnoxious way is clueless rather than mean-
spirited. They're puzzled and would actually appreciate being told
how they come across to others.

In any case, we are informally rewarding and punishing people,
encouraging and discouraging them, praising and criticizing them,
all the time. And of course, parents and teachers, and the community
as a whole, all have a big role in bringing up kids and molding their
characters. They use praise and criticism, rewards and discipline, to
do this. So what Professor Ishida means when she talks about a society that abides by the moral system is that in such a society there's
a strong tendency for moral behavior—that is, behavior directed
toward avoiding harms to others and helping those who need it—to
be respected, encouraged, and rewarded in these sorts of informal
ways. And immoral behavior would be discouraged and punished,
again in all sorts of informal ways.

CHARLIE: But how could humans ever live in this morally good
society without being forced to be moral?

BEN: Remember that it's a hypothetical exercise. The deliberative
committee imagines a society in which morality just *is* the general

practice, as opposed to something that's forced on people. In thinking through what it would be like to live under the moral system, it's not required that the deliberative committee imagine a society in which everyone is morally perfect. No society is like that, and every individual human being makes some moral mistakes. But even in the world as it actually is, you can see real differences in different societies regarding the degree to which morality is respected and practiced. In some, corruption is widespread and treated with a wink and a nod. Civil servants won't do anything for anyone unless bribed; citizens feel like it's OK to break the law or cheat on their taxes, and good behavior isn't really encouraged or expected. In some societies, people are mistreated because of their religious beliefs, ethnicity, race, or gender. Again, no society is perfect in its treatment of minorities and women, but some are a lot better than others. In some societies, rudeness is simply taken for granted, but in others politeness is valued and respected. Some people think that in these days of smartphones and other digital distractions, people in our society have become more rude than they used to be, for example texting instead of interacting with the person who is talking to them, so that you can hardly have an uninterrupted conversation with anyone anymore.

CHRISTINE: OK, I plead guilty to that. I find myself doing it even though I get annoyed when others do it to me.

SHARIFA: Me too. But this conversation is too interesting to be interrupted.

*The others laugh as Sharifa and Christine pull out their phones and turn them off.*

BEN: But of course there are many moral differences among societies regarding public behavior that have nothing to do with technology. For example, many have noted how British society strongly values public politeness and mutual respect. They've informally developed the system of queuing—politely waiting one's turn in line—instead of all crowding, pushing, and shoving to get onto a bus, for example. There's no law about queuing, and police don't force people to stand in line. It's just a culture of politeness that evolved in that society and has become part of the British national character.

And you have parts of the U.S. where people are friendlier and more respectful than in other places. There are small towns and neighborhoods where people don't need to lock their doors or their bikes. In other places, your bike wouldn't last five minutes left unlocked.

So in thinking of a society that operates under the moral system, the deliberative committee would be thinking of a hypothetical but realistically possible society in which social norms tend toward respect for the rules of morality, corruption among public officials and civil servants is not a huge problem even if occasional instances do occur, and prominent people who act morally are admired and those who don't are disapproved of. People take seriously ideas of justice and fairness. Parenting attitudes and educational policies favor instilling as habits in children things like respect for others, learning not to be rude, learning to control one's temper, and so on. It's a society where people recognize the value of such ways of treating each other and act morally out of habit, training, and interpersonal expectation.

CHARLIE: Some people think that all this civilizing is a bad thing. It dulls people's creative spirit.

BEN: Nietzsche, for example. One of the points of the deliberative committee is to see how a rejection of morality such as that expressed in some of Nietzsche's work fares when the options are all carefully laid out for members of the committee to consider and choose from.

CHRISTINE: But how would these people on the deliberative committee ever reach any agreement? If the deliberative committee is open to all sorts of individuals, it's going to have religious believers like Matt and Sharifa and atheists like Charlie. I don't see how you're ever going to get them to agree on one system to govern everyone.

BEN: One way some philosophers have tried to achieve agreement is by restricting what deliberators can know. Professor Ishida's idea for the deliberative committee comes out of a tradition of ethical theorists who think that the nature of morality or justice can be better understood if we imagine reflective individuals in dialogue with each other—philosophers like Thomas Hobbes, Jürgen Habermas, John Rawls, David Gautier, and Bernard Gert. In order that potential bias or self-interest be taken out of the deliberative mix, Rawls and Gert imagine deliberators who have to make their decisions not knowing about their actual gender, race, or social status in the real world. Rawls talks about it as the "veil of ignorance," Gert as the "blindfold of justice." Gert's blindfold is a bit less restrictive than Rawls' veil in that it allows deliberators to know what their own particular rankings of good things are—that is, they know what sorts of things they most value in life and how they would rank them in terms of their degree of personal meaningfulness or importance. Professor Ishida's conception is even more open than Gert's, since in her scenario the deliberators don't operate behind any blindfold or veil. They just bring their actual existing knowledge of themselves, their social status, and their rankings of good things to the deliberative table. This makes the exercise much less abstract than it is under Rawls or Gert. People thinking about the hypothetical deliberative committee can simply imagine themselves—just as they are—as deliberators in dialogue with other people as they know *them* to be.

MATT: But that means that the deliberators aren't necessarily impartial the way they are under Rawls' veil of ignorance, for example.

BEN: Right. But Professor Ishida thinks that, in regard to something like justifying morality, the consequences of this are not as troublesome as has been thought and that in any case it's very useful and revealing to run the exercise in this open way.

The only constraints Professor Ishida puts on her deliberative procedures are that individuals on the committee must have the ordinary intelligence to reason and deliberate—they don't have to be geniuses or "moral experts"—that they can't be required to endorse some system that it would be irrational for them to endorse, and that they can't just agree to disagree. They each have to actively participate in the deliberations by putting forward for discussion their actual values and beliefs (which may, of course, change in the course of the deliberative proceedings themselves). Lack of resolution can occur if for every system considered, it's irrational for at least one deliberator to endorse that system. Suppose that there's just one system that it's not irrational for any deliberator to endorse. Then the committee as a whole must endorse that system. Gert calls this public endorsement, because the committee members are acknowledging publicly to the others on the committee that it's not irrational for them to put this system forward as the one that would govern society from that point on.

Professor Ishida acknowledges that a committee organized under these deliberative procedures does not provide the unanimous and clear-cut results that some of the other philosophers I've mentioned seek. But she thinks the results of such deliberations will show that many or most of us will be confronted with compelling arguments to the effect that we ought to both publicly endorse the moral system and do our best to live in accordance with it.

CHRISTINE: You've said that the system agreed to has to be something each member of the deliberative committee can rationally accept. But especially if the deliberators aren't restricted in what they know, that just seems impossible to me. There are a lot of things some people would find irrational that others wouldn't, especially when it comes to something as controversial as morality.

BEN: Professor Ishida, following Gert, defines rationality and irrationality in a quite specific way. She emphasizes that "rational" isn't to be confused with "reasonable." The latter concept has to do with evidence for, or good reasons in support of, a proposition. The terms "rational" and "irrational," by contrast, apply to *actions*. A person's action or potential action is assessed as irrational if undertaking it would significantly harm her interests with no compensating gains to herself.

SHARIFA: So doing something that harms oneself is irrational?

BEN: Not necessarily. A patient could agree to something harmful to herself in the short term—like a painful operation or course of therapy—if it provides her with long-term gains. But a rational action doesn't have to benefit oneself at all. The person doing the action could even know that it would create a long-term harm for herself. For example, it could be rational for a person to willingly give up something significant to herself—her time or wealth or even her life—for the sake of her child. In fact, something like giving up time for the sake of your child is typical of parents, and no one questions its rationality. Even if someone makes sacrifices to someone she doesn't know—say in giving to charity or risking and perhaps losing one's life to save that of a stranger—her action is not irrational if it was motivated by concern for the suffering of others or if done simply out of a sense of duty.

CHARLIE: So then it's the other way around—an action is irrational if it *doesn't* involve some self-sacrifice on behalf of others?

BEN: Not at all. If some misanthrope doesn't care at all about anyone else, it would actually be irrational for him to sacrifice anything significant to help anyone. Gert emphasizes that rationality is not the same as morality. The basic idea is really just that the action is rational if it's congruent with the interests and values of the person acting, whatever those may be. A selfish person who doesn't care about others can be completely rational while doing immoral things that hurt other people. This is the key reason why it becomes a hard philosophical problem to find some rational justification for behaving morally. Some philosophers have argued that being rational entails acting morally. But Gert argues, and Professor Ishida agrees, that this argument doesn't work. You can't extract a requirement to behave morally from considerations of self-interest alone, not even so-called enlightened self-interest. That idea is meant to suggest that if a selfish person goes beyond simply satisfying some immediate desire and thinks instead about his long-term interests, he will see that he should forego immoral pleasures. Sometimes that's true, but not always. In some cases a clever, calculating, and purely self-interested person will have good reason to conclude that his interests are best served over the long term by some immoral course of action.

CHARLIE: There was a guy in my town—very polite, good-natured—worked as a bank teller. No criminal record, went to church. You wouldn't imagine him hurting a fly. But one day, after he'd worked his way up the hierarchy at the bank and got access to the safe, he cleaned it out. Nobody ever heard from him again. I imagine him enjoying life on some South Sea island.

CHRISTINE: I hope he's not your hero, Charlie!
But Ben, I'm trying to figure out from what you're saying what *would* count as an irrational action.

BEN: Gert defines rationality in such a way that almost every intentional action that a normal adult human does is rational. Precisely because people don't have the interest or motivation to do something that would count as irrational for them to do, most actions actually performed are not irrational.

But of course there are a lot of actions that *would* be irrational for a person, given her interests, values, and motivations, if she *did* perform them. Suppose someone hates opera, has no desire to hear opera for its own sake and no extrinsic motivation for attending operas (an extrinsic motivation might be wanting to impress others as being a high-class sophisticate or perhaps just to accommodate a friend who loves opera). Then it would be irrational for that person to spend any time going to operas. And precisely for that reason, you won't find them choosing to go.

CHRISTINE: What's the point of talking about these kinds of actions that people almost never do?

BEN: They have a very useful role to play in thinking about the deliberative scenarios used by Gert and Professor Ishida. Given Gert's concept of an irrational action, it will turn out that a lot of the systems for organizing society that might be considered by the deliberative committee would be ruled out of court, because it would be irrational for some or all of the deliberators to endorse that system.

Take a system that makes me—Ben Prescott—dictator of the world and able to do anything I want with impunity, while all other people must devote themselves to catering to my needs and desires. It would be irrational for anyone, except perhaps myself, to agree to live under that system. They would have their freedom restricted and could be harmed by me, with no compensating gains for themselves—because I wouldn't have to promise them anything in return for their service to me, and I wouldn't be punished for harming them.

Even many systems of a more general nature—systems that don't refer to one specific individual—would be irrational for most if not all deliberators to accept. Consider a system that privileges people by height, so that there would be rules like "The shorter person must accommodate all the demands of any taller person," "Taller people can never be punished for harming shorter people," and so on. It would certainly be irrational for a short person to agree to this system. Even most tall people would find this irrational to agree to. In addition to having to worry about those who are even taller than they are, there will typically be a lot of short people they know and care about—and not just their young children—whom they would not like to see suffer from this sort of discriminatory system.

CHARLIE: But how would the tall people find that this is irrational? Wouldn't they at least have some compensating benefits, given
the deference shorter people would have to pay to them?

BEN: They might receive benefits, but, in the case of a tall person
with fairly typical values and interests, those benefits wouldn't compensate for their losses, given their concerns about harm to others
whom they care about, about the discriminatory nature of the system,
and so on. Of course, some individual tall persons might care only
about the benefits they receive, and not about the harms to others.
So it might not be irrational for them to accept this system. But most
people aren't that heartless.

Rawls and Gert can claim that their deliberative scenarios will result
in unanimous agreement because of the restrictions they place on what
a deliberator can know about herself. Professor Ishida's open deliberative structure doesn't have this result. Some deliberators will find it
irrational to publicly endorse the moral system. But she thinks that this
is itself an instructive result. She thinks that we can look for underlying
patterns in cases where individuals cannot rationally endorse morality
and that the reasons for such failures to endorse morality can, at least in
some cases, provide further support for the moral system.

MATT: So Professor Ishida's scenario differs from those of Rawls
and Gert in that she allows deliberators to keep all their knowledge
about themselves. Is that the only difference?

BEN: No. The deliberations as Professor Ishida structures them
have two parts, with two questions asked. The first question is the
same as the question asked in Gert's deliberative scenario: What system, if any, would the deliberators, in their conversations among
themselves, find themselves rationally required to publicly endorse?
What both Gert and Professor Ishida think is that the deliberators will
(with only a few exceptions in the case of Professor Ishida's structure)
be rationally required to endorse the moral system over all non-moral
alternatives.

But this first question concerning public agreement still leaves
unaddressed what a deliberator might privately resolve to do. So the
second question in Professor Ishida's scenario is whether a deliberator
would decide to do her best to comply, in the conduct of her personal
life, with the system publicly endorsed.

Gert's justification of morality concerns only the question of public endorsement. But Professor Ishida is interested in what arguments would be available to typical deliberators concerning whether they should intend to personally comply with the guidelines of the system they have publicly endorsed. In principle, a deliberator could publicly endorse the moral system but then resolve to follow a self-interested, anti-moral path in her actual conduct. Professor Ishida thinks that, given typical beliefs and attitudes, many or most deliberators will find that the reasons supporting their own personal compliance with morality will be stronger than the reasons they have for a general personal policy to behave immorally.

CHARLIE: So the idea is that you could take someone like me, and also Christine, Sharifa, and Matt here, with all our different beliefs and different worldviews—different religions or attitudes toward religion, different beliefs about the objectivity of morality, and so on—and find that we would all agree among ourselves that objective universal morality trumps all other possibilities? It seems like a tall order to me.

BEN: So it is. Professor Ishida does acknowledge that the result of her thought experiment is not everything some philosophers have claimed or hoped for in terms of providing a justification for morality. For one thing, it doesn't show that a requirement to be moral can be derived from considerations of rationality alone—something, as I've noted, some philosophers have claimed or hoped for. A second limitation in her justification stems from the fact that she doesn't use a veil of ignorance or blindfold within her hypothetical deliberative structure. This means that her deliberators know who they are and what their social situation is. When they have such knowledge, there will be exceptional circumstances in which it will not be rational for some deliberators to even publicly endorse the moral system, let alone comply with it.

More positively, here's what she thinks her deliberative structure *will* show: that the non-moral systems are such that the committee as a whole would be rationally required to reject them, and that almost everyone will find themselves rationally required to publicly endorse the moral system. Going beyond public endorsement to the question of private compliance with morality, she thinks her deliberative scenario will show that many or most members of the committee will find that the arguments available to them saying that they should do their best to privately comply with the moral system will be stronger than the arguments they will have for refusing to comply. Even with her deliberative structure's limitations, I think that if she can make the case that it achieves these two positive goals, she's accomplished a lot. At any rate, it's something you should be able to test, because I'm sure she would think that all of you would find yourselves giving positive, morality-supporting answers to both questions, once you've worked through her deliberative scenario.

CHARLIE: OK, count me skeptical, but I'm eager to see how this works.

MATT: Me too, and I think the rest of us concur. Let's see what this comes to.

# The Moral System

CHRISTINE: So Professor Ishida thinks that her deliberative committee thought experiment can show that almost everyone would publicly endorse the moral system. Ben, you've given us a general description of the moral system and compared it with religious systems and moral relativism. But we've been seeing in class that different philosophers who support morality have different ideas about what exactly the moral system is. How does that work into what the deliberators are deciding on?

BEN: Good question. Professor Ishida wants to keep things as simple as possible in talking about the justification of morality. Her project is not to show that some one specific version of the moral system is superior to competing versions. The theory of Utilitarianism, for example, assesses the morality of actions by looking at their consequences and at the amount of happiness—or unhappiness—they generate in society. Kantianism, by contrast, evaluates actions by considering whether the reasons for an action come under a rule that one could consistently or reasonably accept everyone following. These theories will disagree in their moral assessments of some actions in some cases. But they have the same broad aims and share key features with other moral systems. Professor Ishida's justification of morality claims that a system with these key features will be favored by deliberators over non-moral systems, all of which lack one or more of these features and which have additional features that become problematic in terms of what deliberators can rationally endorse.

MATT: OK. So what are these key features?

BEN: One feature is that the principles for regulating behavior are universal and impartial—they apply equally to everyone—and that they are timeless—they apply to every era. This means that they cannot be changed or overturned by some authoritarian decree, legislative fiat, or cultural change. A second feature is that the individuals to whom these principles apply are assumed to have a capacity for deliberative choice. It's only because someone can deliberate and choose freely among her options that she can be held morally responsible for the choices she makes. Third, the principles make at least some categorical judgments to the effect that an action or type of action is acceptable or unacceptable (some moral systems may allow for some indeterminacy about some cases). Perhaps the central feature concerns what these principles are about—their content. They can be broadly described as having the aim of encouraging behaviors that benefit others and discouraging, including punishing, behaviors that are harmful to others. Finally, there's what one might call the "other-regarding" feature of moral systems. This is an implication of the impartiality of the principles. The principles apply to every person generally, without favoring or disfavoring a particular individual or group. So, in order to abide by these principles, each person must accord at least minimal respect to every other person he interacts with. In particular, one person is not allowed to harm, manipulate, or interfere with another without a justifiable reason, where self-interest by itself cannot count as such a reason.

Professor Ishida thinks that these general features are what deliberators on her committee will be rationally required to publicly endorse. Since all the genuine moral systems, like Kantianism, Utilitarianism, and Gert's account of common morality, share these features, her justification of morality doesn't require adjudicating among them or resolving those cases in which two moral theories will make different judgments regarding the morality of some specific type of action. For convenience she sometimes talks about *the* moral system, a covering term referring to any system with the above features. She uses it with the understanding that even if, as she thinks, morality is justified over non-moral alternatives, there are still many debates about the morality of specific types of actions left unresolved after the deliberative committee has done its work.

CHRISTINE: Going back to that first feature—the idea of timeless principles that can't be changed sounds so inflexible and absolutist to me.

BEN: It's understandable that things can look that way from this brief description. But it turns out that specific moral theories can have these general features I've mentioned yet allow for a surprising degree of sensitivity to specific circumstances, so that an action that's morally unacceptable in one circumstance is acceptable in another.

Moral theories can also respect some differences in cultural beliefs and practices.

SHARIFA: You mean like Professor Ishida's example concerning acceptable differences in moral assessments of Japanese and American conversational practices?

BEN: That's right.

MATT: You've mentioned that there are different versions of moral systems, like Kantianism and Utilitarianism. So aren't religions examples of moral systems too?

BEN: Religion is distinct from morality. Among other differences, religions have additional features not belonging to moral systems—features that mean that they will be treated differently from moral systems in the deliberative scenario.

MATT: You've already said that sometimes religion can become an enemy of morality. I don't think you really mean to say that religions are immoral, but sometimes you make it sound that way.

BEN: No, I'm not making any such general claim about religion. In fact, much of what religion teaches is held in common with what morality teaches. And religion has had an important role—perhaps an essential one—in human history in supporting and encouraging moral behavior in people. But a religion typically goes beyond what morality proper is about. Morality is secular in the sense that it doesn't presuppose a deity. Religions have a web of beliefs—each set of beliefs pretty idiosyncratic to that religion—about the existence and nature of their God. And there are a lot of rules about how to worship that God. These aren't moral rules. Morality itself doesn't say anything about God.

MATT: But isn't God necessary to enforce morality?

BEN: Perhaps he does enforce it, but the claim that he does is not a claim that the moral system itself makes. Maybe God punishes evil-doers with hell and rewards the morally good with heaven. Or maybe he doesn't exist, and the rewards and punishments that do occur are all meted out by society.

MATT: But society is often unfair in how it rewards and punishes people. Without God, there's no justice.

BEN: Society is often unfair and imperfect. But that doesn't completely eliminate the idea of justice. The moral system tells us how we ought to behave. It doesn't guarantee that society, or the world as a whole, always produces the most just outcome. Part of the problem of course is that people often don't do what morality says they ought to do. But if there is no God, it's presumably better if society does have a system of rewards, permissions, and punishments that it enforces, however imperfectly, than if society had no such system at all. So I don't think you can say there's *no* justice without God, only that social attempts to create a just society are imperfect, to greater and lesser degrees in different societies.

MATT: But you're still supposing that morality could exist without God. Didn't Dostoevsky say, "If God does not exist, then everything is permitted"?

BEN: Some people may believe that. They imagine that if there were no God, or if people did not believe in God, they would run amok and just do whatever they felt like, because they wouldn't fear God's wrath or worry about ending up in hell. But the claim that Dostoevsky's characters discuss in *The Brothers Karamazov* just seems false on empirical grounds. Society may not be perfect, but it does play the role that God is said to play—whether in addition to God or instead of God doesn't matter for our present purposes. Society forbids some behaviors like murder, and murderers are severely punished. Society also has many systems of rewards, from words of praise from a parent or teacher to medals, monetary rewards, promotions, and so on.

And people are clearly motivated by these social systems of reward and punishment. I'm sure, too, that there are secular people who care about morality for its own sake, without thinking in terms of rewards and punishments. It may be that religious people are on balance better behaved than nonbelievers, but if so it's a subtle thing. There is an increasing percentage of people in contemporary society who don't believe in God, but I suspect you'd have a hard time picking them out of a crowd in terms of comparing the morality of their behaviors with those of religious people. Clearly, many nonbelievers value kindness and try to be kind and try not to hurt others, even if they don't believe that there will be rewards and punishments in the afterlife. They teach their children to be good.

They're happy, and full of praise for them, when their children behave morally and are disappointed and punish them when they don't do so well.

It remains to be seen whether trends away from religious belief will continue. But it's surely possible in principle to have a largely secular society that nevertheless respects morality.

CHRISTINE: I guess I understand these general features that you've said the specific moral theories all have in common. But it would be nice to have something a little more concrete to think about.

BEN: Sure. Professor Ishida particularly likes the moral system as articulated by Bernard Gert. Gert thinks that precisely because morality is a universal system held in common, and independently of religious belief, its basic nature has to be relatively straightforward and understandable by every moral agent. So Gert's system can serve as a good stand-in for other, typically more complex accounts of morality, like Kantianism or Utilitarianism.

CHRISTINE: What's a moral agent?

BEN: Someone who is capable of deliberating and acting on the basis of reasons, not just blindly or instinctually. Moral agents have the capacity to reflect on their behavior and to choose among their options. In saying someone is a moral agent, we're not saying that the person is necessarily acting morally—rather that they are *capable* of acting morally—and immorally as well. It's moral agents, and only moral agents, who can be held morally responsible for their actions. Nonhuman animals, most of them at least, are not moral agents. An ant can't be blamed, or praised for that matter, for killing an enemy ant. It's just how they are programmed to treat intruders. Babies are not moral agents, nor are very young children. By middle childhood, we hold children somewhat but not fully responsible for their actions. They have begun to understand the idea of acting a certain way because it's the right thing to do, not just because they've been told to or because they'll be punished if they don't. But they don't yet have enough self-control to be fully capable of choosing on the basis of moral deliberations. The development of moral agency is a gradual thing, but it's something mentally sound adult humans possess.

So in terms of a specific moral theory that can make our reflections more concrete, here's the set of moral rules Professor Ishida wants us to look at—I've got copies of the handout for our next class. It's from Bernard Gert's book *Common Morality*:

1. Do not kill.
2. Do not cause pain.
3. Do not disable.
4. Do not deprive of freedom.
5. Do not deprive of pleasure.
6. Do not deceive.
7. Keep your promises.
8. Do not cheat.
9. Obey the law.
10. Do your duty.

These moral rules are primarily concerned with preventing harms to others or reducing the likelihood of harm. In addition to the moral rules, there are moral ideals like kindness and charity that have the aim of benefiting others. Common morality, according to Gert, includes these rules and ideals, and also procedures for making moral judgments in specific cases, including those situations when following one rule might require breaking another. In saying that morality is common, Gert doesn't mean that everyone *explicitly* understands this system; but he does think that people do *implicitly* understand it, much like people have an implicit understanding of grammatically correct and incorrect sentences in their native language, even if they can't explicitly articulate the grammatical structures and rules of their language.

MATT: What does that final moral rule "Do your duty" mean? Isn't that just a repeat of the idea that you should do what is morally right?

BEN: No. For Gert it just means you ought to fulfill the responsibilities of the specific roles you have in life. So if you're a parent, you have a duty to care for your child, or at least to see that the child gets adequate care from others, for example, if the parents decide to give a baby up for adoption. If you have a job, you should fulfill the requirements of the job as they're outlined by a contract or by what the boss asks you to do.

CHRISTINE: What if the boss asks you to do something morally questionable, like my boyfriend's boss who wants him to cut corners when they refill print cartridges?

BEN: I guess that duty stops when one is asked to do something immoral. In general, Gert thinks that all these rules can be justifiably broken or violated in some circumstances. He offers a set of secondary rules explaining when a violation of a basic moral rule is morally acceptable. Professor Ishida gave an example in class in which it seems pretty uncontroversial that it's morally OK to break a moral rule: Say I'm a doctor who made a promise to meet my colleague for lunch. On the way there, I come across an accident victim whom I can help. But it takes time and means I have to miss my lunch appointment. In a case like this, it seems obvious that I ought to violate the rule not to break promises in order to help save the life of the accident victim.

Or you can break the rules "Do not cause pain" and "Do not deprive of freedom" when you take your child—who wants to exercise his freedom to keep playing basketball—to the doctor to get a shot. Your child is unhappy on both counts. You've deprived him of freedom and you've caused him pain. But everyone would agree that it's OK to cause some short-term pain and a brief deprivation of freedom for the sake of your child's long-term health. That's part of your moral duty as a parent. Any reasonable version of the moral system has to offer an account of the sorts of conditions under which it can be OK to violate the moral rule about not hurting people.

CHRISTINE: When you noted those general features that moral systems have in common, you included that moral principles were impartial. Does that mean I'm expected to treat everyone the same? I can't show a little partiality toward my friends?

BEN: Advocates of different moral theories will disagree about the extent to which our moral obligations depend on our relatedness to specific other people. Most specific accounts of our moral obligations hold that you will have stronger obligations to your family and immediate community than to those at a distance, while some forms of Utilitarianism emphasize that, especially these days with our technology and instant access to knowledge about conditions around the world, we do better by helping those much worse off than we and those in our community are. But what all moral systems share in common is impartiality in the sense that everyone is on a par from the point of view of the moral system itself, as it were. The principles of morality don't single out any one person or group for special benefits or harms. From the moral point of view, you and those you care about have the same moral status as everyone else. Everyone is equal under the principles of morality.

So all these moral theories would agree that all moral agents deserve protection from unjustified harms. They treat this claim as a universal, not as culturally relative. If some culture says that an ethnic group or gender falls below the level of such protection, or doesn't have that protection to the degree more privileged moral agents have, that falls afoul of anything a moral system would allow.

CHRISTINE: When you note that moral principles are universal and timeless, that makes the contrast with moral relativism really striking. You've also noted how religious systems can sometimes have immoral teachings or practices. Are there other systems and ideas in opposition to morality?

BEN: There's another system advocated by some that's a little tricky to classify. It's clear that a quite self-centered, egotistical individual who is systematically willing to take advantage of, hurt, or even kill others when it suits his selfish purposes is not acting in accordance with the moral system. Typically such individuals don't act from any principled system of beliefs at all. But there is a theory called ethical egoism that tries to offer a principled defense of this sort of attitude as something that should apply to everyone. Unlike the ordinary egotist, who only cares that his personal desires are satisfied, the theory of ethical egoism says that *everyone* ought to act only on the basis of his or her own interests. No one has any obligations to anyone outside themselves and their own orbit of concern. So is this another ethical theory, alongside Kantianism and Utilitarianism? It is often treated as such, because it shares some of the features common to moral theories. It is intended to offer a universally true prescription for everyone's behavior, and it is structurally similar to Utilitarianism.

But ethical egoism fails what I called the "other-regarding" feature of genuinely moral systems. It does not acknowledge that every moral agent should be treated with equal respect in terms of not having the common rules of morality violated against them. It allows someone to think just about himself and any specific individuals he cares about, whereas morality requires that you take everyone into account, not necessarily to the extent of extending benefits to them but at least to the extent of not manipulating or harming them without regard to anything but your own interests. In a genuinely moral system, the fact that you may not care about them doesn't give you the right to harm them. So-called ethical egoism, therefore, really isn't very ethical. This doesn't mean that it is excluded from consideration by the deliberative committee. But ethical egoism counts as a criticism of and an alternative to genuinely moral systems, rather than an example of a moral system.

CHRISTINE: Is morality just about helping and not harming those who are moral agents? You said that young children were not moral agents. I'm sure you're not saying it's OK to kill toddlers!

BEN: Of course not. Specific moral theories may disagree to some extent about why this is so—is it because they are loved by moral agents, or because they will *become* moral agents, or simply because they are human beings? Actually, it doesn't have to be just one factor; it could be a combination of these reasons. Specific moral theories will disagree about how far this moral respect for non-moral agents extends. Whether it extends to human fetuses is a core question disputed in the abortion debate. Moral vegetarians insist that it extends to at least some nonhuman animals. And so on.

CHRISTINE: Here are those debates again that suggest something like relativism to me.

BEN: Right. And they are important debates. But Professor Ishida thinks that we can learn a lot about morality and its critics without having to resolve all these specific moral debates.

MATT: Aren't there still other anti-moral beliefs and attitudes, such as racism?

BEN: Yes. Racism is an example of a social structure that systematically deprives groups of moral agents of their moral rights. Similar deprivations to the relevant groups occur in sexist and ethnocentric societies. One can also talk about ways in which the formal laws of a society can run afoul of morality—for example, when they legalize racist or sexist discrimination. There are parallels here with our discussion of the relation between religion and morality. It's not that either law or religion is usually, or by intent, immoral. But both are independent systems, distinct from the moral system and from each other, of course. So one can identify immoral laws as well as immoral religious teachings.

However, any society that can be said to be following the moral system will be one that includes formal laws and legal institutions within it. Serious offenses against morality require significant punishments. This in turn requires laws that make clear what these offenses are, a police force to enforce these laws, and a court system to try to ensure that those accused of serious offenses have indeed committed them.

But the most distinctive part of the moral system will be the set of informal guidelines that go beyond formal laws and legislation. Proponents of morality want to encourage helpful and generous behavior but, beyond perhaps some minor requirements, it would not be reasonable to make such behavior a *legal* obligation on everyone. Nor would it be morally acceptable to punish less serious offenses against morality with fines and jail terms. In fact, most of the ways in which we act immorally toward one another are best addressed by informal punishments and criticisms.

CHARLIE: You've said that law and religion are basically complementary to morality, even if they conflict with morality in some specific cases. But is there some theory that completely rejects morality, and maybe religion and the law too?

BEN: Moral nihilism holds that there just is no such thing as morality. It's pretty closely related to relativism in that both reject the idea of any universal morality. But nihilism is more radical in suggesting that the whole idea of morality—even within a society— is a sham. Relativism at least allows that there can be moral truths. According to cultural relativism, it's true that, within a culture, some actions are morally right—those approved by that culture—and others morally wrong. But nihilism denies that anything is morally right or morally wrong anywhere. It's kind of like the property of being a unicorn—you can describe unicorns or believe in them, but there's nothing that really has that property. You're just wrong if you believe in unicorns and, according to the moral nihilist, you're just wrong if you believe in any moral truths. Moral nihilism sees morality as a kind of false ideology that oppressive governments or religions use to keep people in line.

So these are the major ways in which morality can be criticized or in which non-moral institutions and systems can conflict with the moral system. Professor Ishida's deliberative structure is meant to allow us to assess these criticisms and to compare and evaluate the moral system in contrast to the non-moral alternatives to it.

# The Deliberative Committee, Ethical Egoism, and Authenticity

CHARLIE: So I've been thinking about how Professor Ishida has structured the rules for her deliberative committee, and I see how that structure leads to one result Ben has already touched on: It's clear that it would be irrational for everyone else on the deliberative committee to endorse a society in which Ben Prescott is dictator of the world and everyone is forced to cater to him. Ditto, I guess, for a society in which Charlie Emerson is the dictator—although that one sounds better to me!

CHRISTINE: We like you better the way you are, Charlie!

CHARLIE: But what about a society based on the theory you mentioned, Ben, in which the rule is that everyone is equal in their right to look out for themselves? Ethical egoism, I think you called it. You said it was something the deliberative committee could consider. And it seems fair. It's not putting me above everyone else. You look out for yourself and your interests just as I look out for myself and my interests. I let you go your way if you let me go mine. Everybody benefits because each is granted the freedom to live the way he or she wants to.

And what you're saying, Ben, is that someone like myself, as a member of the deliberative committee, is going to be rationally required to endorse the moral system, instead of ethical egoism. I just don't see that.

BEN: Let's not even talk about someone *like* you. Professor Ishida encourages you to think of yourselves as deliberators—just as you are with your existing values and beliefs.

CHARLIE: OK, it should be easy to figure out what I believe! So I say that it would *not* be rational for me to accept the moral system, because I disagree with it. I think ethical egoism is better.

BEN: But the question that matters here isn't about what theory you prefer. It's about what it would be irrational or rational for you

and others to publicly endorse in the specific context of the deliberative committee and its rules for reaching an agreement. Remember
that we're looking for a system that everyone on the deliberative
committee would find it rational to publicly endorse. So Sharifa,
Christine, Matt—what do you say? Would it be rational for you to
agree to a system like Charlie has described, where each person is
allowed equal freedom to live the way they want to without being
bound by any other person's rules or preferences?

SHARIFA: What if the way someone wants to live is harmful to
me? It could be something as trivial, but annoying, as listening to loud
music when I want to sleep, or as harmful as stealing from me, or
lying to me or cheating me in order to get what they want.

CHARLIE: Well, you'd have to have some limits—like "Live the
way you want to live as long as you aren't harming someone else."

SHARIFA: But then you start getting something like the rules of
morality—don't hurt others, don't lie or cheat, and so on.

CHRISTINE: That's right. And if the setup for an ethical egoist
society is that there would be no punishments for doing something
"wrong" because the society doesn't really define things as right or
wrong except in terms of an individual's self-interests, then no one
would be punished even for killing someone, assuming that the killer
was acting in his own self-interest.

CHARLIE: Well, it would be in the guy's self-interest not to kill
because he would be punished.

BEN: But that's just it. If it were really a society that followed
ethical egoism, then he wouldn't be punished, because the theory
says that you are acting acceptably if you act in your self-interest. And
the whole society would be organized around that idea—that's what
ethical egoism is saying.

CHARLIE: OK, I see what you're getting at. But let me be devil's
advocate for a bit, because I want to think about all the implications
of this. Suppose I said that I don't care if murderers aren't punished
under this system, because I'd kill anyone who tried to kill me.

SHARIFA: Maybe you'd be strong enough to fight someone
off, but what if you weren't? Or what about your grandparents? If

you accumulated a lot of wealth, a bunch of thieves might conspire together to overpower you. Under this ethical egoist system, there would be no rules against doing that and no punishment for doing it.

CHARLIE: If I was wealthy enough, I could hire bodyguards to protect me and my parents and grandparents, and kids when I have them, as well as my possessions.

CHRISTINE: I really don't like the look of the sort of society you're describing, Charlie. Given that there are no formal or informal societal restrictions to prevent people from doing whatever is in their own interests, wealthy people will hire bodyguards to protect their families and property. But they might then enjoy using this power to acquire more wealth. Then the less powerful are either at the mercy of these wealthy people, or they find some way to put themselves under their protection, presumably by doing things for the wealthy people. It sounds like a feudal or even warlord type of society. Not for me!

SHARIFA: And Charlie, there you are sitting on the deliberative committee. You're a college student, not particularly wealthy as far as I know . . .

CHARLIE: "Not particularly wealthy" is the understatement of the decade! I've got negative wealth! Given my student loans, every day I'm in college I have a little more negative wealth than I did the day before.

SHARIFA: So then in this system, without wealth, how do you propose to protect yourself and your family from those with power? Are you ready to become a vassal of someone else who can protect you? And if not, would it really be rational for you to endorse this ethical egoist system?

CHARLIE: Well, I've sort of seen this coming, but no—it wouldn't be rational for me to choose to live in the society this is starting to look like. It would put me at too many disadvantages. It's not really in my interests to spend time and energy trying to set up my zone of safety and defend it against other, maybe more powerful individuals who would feel free to take anything of mine they can get. And even if I knew that I was wealthy, I still don't see it as something

I would really choose. It would be a survival of the fittest situation. I think Christine is right that it looks pretty grim and scary. And I'm not a misanthrope. I have friends I care about. I like the thought of having kids some day. What kind of legacy would I leave them if I gave them a society like that? As an initial idea, the ethical egoist system sounds pretty good—it sounds fair and it seems to offer a kind of freedom that would potentially benefit everyone. But I hadn't really thought it through.

SHARIFA: I'm glad to hear you say that, Charlie. But even if you *were* the sort of person who didn't care about hurting others—even if you found it rational, given your values, to endorse the ethical egoist system, it wouldn't be rational for *me* to endorse it. It would offer nothing for me in terms of my values. It would only provide threats to my well-being. So by the deliberative committee's procedures, the ethical egoist proposal couldn't get off the ground anyway.

BEN: Which is to say that this ethical egoism approach—the idea that each person should live according to their own interests and desires with no restrictions or punishments if the exercise of those interests and desires harms others—is not a plausible candidate for approval by the deliberative committee.

Professor Ishida would make an additional point: It's not surprising that it would not be rational for others to endorse the system put forward by the ethical egoist, because it would simply make them vulnerable to people who would not be constrained by any rules except self-interest and might therefore harm them. Another result is more surprising: It would *not* be irrational for the ethical egoist—even one who doesn't care about the legacy to his children in the way that Charlie does—to agree to endorse the moral system. In fact, endorsing the moral system gives the egoist significant advantages. The moral system helps protect him from threats to himself and those—if any—that he cares about. It helps protect him from attacks or restrictions on his freedom by others that would go unpunished under the ethical egoist system. His decision to endorse the moral system as a member of the deliberative committee only concerns the act of publicly endorsing the moral system. It does not require him to actually behave morally once he is living under the moral system. He might intend to act selfishly whenever he thinks he can get away with it.

The result is that, for any ethical egoists on the deliberative committee, they will themselves find it irrational to endorse the general system that would put ethical egoism in place, and they will find it rational to endorse the moral system.

CHRISTINE: But wait! In Professor Ishida's deliberative committee, unlike in Rawls' veil of ignorance, everyone knows who they are and what their character, social position, talents, and resources are in real life. Some ethical egoist who knows he's in a powerful position and who doesn't care about hurting others in order to get his way might find it irrational to agree to the moral system. If he reasonably thought that the constraints of the moral system would limit him and offer him no compensating gains, then it might be irrational for him to endorse it.

BEN: There may be some such individuals, and if so, you're right—it would be irrational for them to endorse the moral system.

CHRISTINE: So then the deliberative experiment fails?

BEN: This is where Professor Ishida emphasizes the practical nature of her account. It may be that there are some individuals in psychologically and socially unusual situations who would find it irrational to publicly endorse morality, because they are so powerful in their existing social situation that they can reasonably believe that they can successfully keep others from harming them. But individuals like that are surely few and far between. Such a person would have to have just the right combination of psychological traits and social power: misanthropy—strong disregard for the many people he knows he is harming—a strong, controlling personality, and a dominating social standing that allows him to reasonably believe that he can remain as the top dog into the indefinite future. Anyone with any knowledge of human history, even or especially including knowledge about societies in which morality is not respected or widely practiced, knows that the prospects for the successful long-term endurance of such a tyrant—for that is what such a person is—are not particularly good.

MATT: But I suspect that a lot of tyrants believe that they're a special case and that past history won't apply to them.

BEN: True, but that actually further supports the point that there aren't likely to be many real-world cases in which it would be irrational for someone like this to endorse the moral system. As Matt suggests, many of the individuals who fit the social and psychological profile of a tyrant are pretty arrogant and narcissistic—they aren't actually as powerful and invulnerable as they believe themselves to be. And Gert's concept of rational and irrational action is objective in the sense that individuals can make mistaken assessments regarding what's rational or irrational for them. A deluded person might believe that a course of action is rational for him when in fact it's not. So a tyrant who's unrealistic about his ability to maintain his power might be mistaken in his belief that it's rational for him to endorse the ethical egoist system and irrational to endorse the moral system.

The practical point is that very few individuals could reasonably conclude that it would be irrational to publicly endorse morality if their hesitation in doing so concerns their personally favoring an ethical egoist system. Each of us here, we've now concluded, would be rationally required to endorse the moral system over ethical egoism. And I suspect this would apply to every person you know well enough that you would be able to make a judgment about what they would decide as a deliberator, including those who are initially sympathetic to ethical egoism. This is a pretty powerful result.

CHRISTINE: But then what about your point that even if almost every ethical egoist is rationally required to *endorse* the moral system in his role as a member of the deliberative committee, he's still being rational to intend to pursue his own selfish ends while living under that moral system? He could even decide while he's on the committee something like, "Sure, I have to endorse the moral system because it's rational for me to do that and it's irrational for non-egoists to endorse ethical egoism. But I don't actually have to plan to act morally myself under the moral system, as long as I can avoid getting punished. In fact, I can use others' good behavior in the moral system to my advantage. So that's what I'll do."

This seems completely unfair, but I don't see what's wrong with it under Professor Ishida's setup.

BEN: It is unfair. But no setup can guarantee that everyone acts morally, even in a society that operates under the moral system. That, in fact, is part of the realism of Professor Ishida's deliberative structure. She's not imagining some moral utopia that no human society ever has or ever could achieve.

But we don't have to concede that the typical ethical egoist will not personally comply with the system that she has publicly endorsed. It turns out that many of those who come into the deliberative process favoring ethical egoism, and even many of those who just have straightforwardly egotistical and self-centered personalities, will find most compelling the arguments that they should comply with the moral system in their personal behavior, and not merely endorse it in public.

In order to talk about good arguments for personally complying with the moral system, I should first say something about the basic idea of a good, or reasonable, argument. As I noted earlier, Professor Ishida makes an important distinction between "rational" and "reasonable." This is something of a technical distinction that she and some other philosophers make use of. In ordinary usage, these terms are often interchangeable. But to understand what Professor Ishida is getting at, it's important to keep in mind that she's giving these terms clearly differentiated meanings. We've already seen that her definition of a rational action is very broad, so that almost everything a normal person actually does is rational, and that "rational" and "irrational" apply, in her usage, only to a person's actions. "Reasonable" and "unreasonable," by contrast, apply to the quality of an argument, or to the evidence for a belief. If an argument is reasonable for a person, it's one that the person ought to accept—he ought to believe the conclusion.

CHARLIE: You say an argument is reasonable "for a person," as though it were subjective. But we discussed arguments in logic class, and I thought that you could make objective assessments of arguments. There are principles of reason and inference that make some arguments valid and others fallacious. Everyone should accept the former and deny the latter. It's not up to the individual.

BEN: There are certainly principles of deductive inference and inductive reasoning that are objective. At the same time, there is a useful understanding of a good argument or good reasoning that has a subjective component to it. This understanding of good argumentation is attentive to the fact that, in order for an individual to be in a position to accept a conclusion as reasonable, she has to understand the objective logical relationships that do obtain, she has to have evidence that appropriately supports the premises of the argument, and she has to understand that her evidence does indeed support the conclusion of the argument.

CHARLIE: I'm not sure I understand.

BEN: Take some obviously objectively solid logical relationship like modus ponens:
Premise 1: If P is true then Q is true.
Premise 2: P is true.
Conclusion: Therefore Q is true.
Everyone should accept that this argument *form* is valid. But this doesn't mean that a specific argument in this form is a good argument for a specific individual. An argument is a good argument for a person S only if S has good reason to accept its conclusion. Suppose that the specific argument in question that has this form is one where at least one of the premises (say the premise that P is true) is something S doesn't have evidence for, whereas another person T does have evidence for it. Then the argument is not a good one for S, though it may be a good one for T. Or again suppose that S doesn't understand what the premise means, whereas T does. Then it can't be a good argument *for* S, even if it's a valid argument with true premises.

Another problem can crop up when the logical or evidential relation between premises and conclusion is more complex. Suppose that S doesn't see that the premises do support the conclusion—it's too complicated for her to understand, at least unless she devotes more study to it. It's not a good argument for her in that case.

CHRISTINE: Could this apply to cultures or historical time frames too, so that what's a good argument in one case is not a good argument in another?

BEN: Yes. For example, in the Middle Ages most people had a good argument for the geocentric hypothesis—the idea that celestial objects were in motion above an unmoving Earth. That's what the observational evidence available to people at the time suggested. You could see the sun, moon, and planets move across the sky. And how could the whole Earth be in motion? Not only was the geocentric hypothesis a reasonable one based on observation, it's also what the leading authorities taught. Of course, we now know that, as further evidence was acquired, that hypothesis didn't hold up. As this new evidence accumulated, including explanations of why the Earth could be in motion even though it doesn't appear to be so, the emerging picture came to support beyond any reasonable doubt the heliocentric hypothesis—that the Earth is in motion, orbiting around the sun. So what was a good argument for the typical person in the Middle Ages is a bad argument for us and vice versa.

In the case of beliefs about how we ought to behave, this means that good and bad arguments can vary depending on an individual's specific beliefs and the evidence for them that they have. So if someone has no evidence that smoking is addictive and cancer causing, they might not have a good argument that they ought to stop smoking, whereas someone with that evidence has a very good argument. Cigarette smoking can be thought of more as a prudential question— a matter of self-interest—than a moral one. But the same point applies to fully moral questions concerning people's interactions with each other.

CHRISTINE: Doesn't that make the reasonableness of moral beliefs depend on subjective factors?

BEN: It does to some extent, but not as much as you might think. Very often the evidence backing up a particular moral belief about the right course of action is objective and available to everyone who cares to look, as the evidence about the dangers of smoking now is. Another objective factor in determining whether an argument is a good one for a person concerns whether the person is ignoring evidence that they already have, refusing to believe what the evidence clearly points to, or failing to seek out evidence that they could readily acquire if only they checked. People often don't want to look for evidence for something they don't want to believe. Maybe they fear they have a serious illness, but instead of having the doctor run tests, they refuse to even see a doctor. Some people react to threats to their worldviews by burying their heads in the sand. But that doesn't absolve them from criticism for holding the typically false beliefs they end up with—for example, that I'm perfectly healthy, or that my spouse won't be hurt if I cheat on her, and so on.

CHARLIE: So as I'm understanding this, an argument is a good one for a person relative to his existing beliefs, to the evidence he currently has, or to the evidence he could readily acquire. And it's subjective to that extent, because different people will have different belief sets and different evidence available to them. But this doesn't mean it's totally subjective, right?

BEN: Right. A totally subjective criterion for a good argument would be that an argument is a good one for Smith if Smith believes it's a good argument. That's not what we're talking about. Others have every right, based on objective criteria, to criticize the way Smith reasons, misuses or ignores the evidence he has, or fails to acquire evidence that's readily available.

CHARLIE: Isn't all this a bit inexact? How available does evidence have to be in order to be "readily" available?

BEN: Yes, it is somewhat inexact. I asked Professor Ishida about this, and she said there's lots of work to be done in this area. But she says that the fact that epistemologists haven't worked this out in every detail shouldn't distract from the recognition that there are clear-cut cases on both sides of the divide. Often, it can be quite clear that the conclusion an individual has reached is properly based on the argument's premises and on that person's background beliefs, the evidence he has for the premises, and so on. Then the argument is a good one for that person. Often, it can be equally clear that an argument is not a good one for a person, for the sorts of reasons I've mentioned.

Professor Ishida thinks that such clear-cut cases are enough to suggest that many or most individuals who go through her deliberative process will end up with objectively good arguments for personally complying with the requirements of the moral system. Whether they *recognize* these arguments as the good ones they are and whether they actually do comply with the moral system as the arguments tell them they should are different questions. An individual can be too emotionally involved in an issue or too ideologically committed to recognize an argument as the good one it in fact is for him. That argument might still be a good one for him, because it provides new evidence, or new inferential links that are understandable to him, that adequately support a conclusion that he ought to accept, whether or not he actually does accept it.

CHARLIE: OK. But now I want to see how this applies to my case. I've agreed that I'm rationally required by the deliberative rules to publicly endorse morality. But you said that for people who start with ethical egoist sympathies as I did, there was also a good argument typically present, not just for publicly endorsing morality but also for personally complying with it. Where does that come in?

BEN: Well, how important would it be to you to act in your own self-interests once the deliberative committee has decided on the moral system? And think here about cases where acting in your self-interests causes harm to other people that the moral system would not count as justifiable harm. That's where the moral system genuinely conflicts with how you might consider behaving. If no one were harmed in your pursuit of some project of yours, then it wouldn't be likely to conflict with the moral system. You'd also want to focus on cases where you reasonably believed that you could get away with your harmful action without punishment. If you were unlikely to get away with it, then self-interest would dictate not doing the harmful thing. So, assuming you could get away with it, would you want to orient your life toward pursuing your self-interests in spite of any problems this creates for others?

CHARLIE: Not if it really involved hurting other people. I couldn't do that. In favoring ethical egoism, I was mostly concerned about ways in which my freedom to live as I wish might get restricted by various rules. The way I happen to like living definitely doesn't involve deliberately hurting people in order to get what I want, or constricting their own freedom.

My original thought was that everyone would be better off under an ethical egoist system. I didn't understand all the implications of what it would be like to live under that system. But I'm seeing something else here too.

BEN: What's that?

CHARLIE: So I'm imagining myself on the deliberative committee and I see that the rest of you, given your values, couldn't rationally endorse ethical egoism. By contrast, it's rational for me to publicly endorse the moral system. So by the deliberative rules, I'm required to endorse it. That tells me something positive about the moral system and something negative about ethical egoism, because I can see that, when Sharifa, Matt, and Christine can't rationally endorse ethical egoism, that's not because of some logical mistake or ideological dogma on their part. But even more telling—given that I'm publicly endorsing the moral system, I couldn't honestly say to myself that it's fine for me to endorse it in public and then privately plan to subvert it when it's in my interests to do so. I've hated hypocrites ever since I can remember, and I couldn't stand the thought of myself becoming one. But if I went against the moral system once I'd publicly endorsed it, that's what I would be. So even if my desires and interests might sometimes get the better of me, when they did I'd feel like the guy who really wants to quit smoking and feels bad about himself when he starts puffing away on another cigarette. I'd feel bad, knowing I would be subverting my own newly adopted standards.

CHRISTINE: That's great, Charlie.

But Ben, what about someone who, unlike Charlie, doesn't care about being a hypocrite?

BEN: Well, if they do care about not hurting others, they're going to not want to publicly endorse ethical egoism, once they fully understand its implications. In having that "do no harm" attitude, they would in effect already be implicitly accepting the moral rules on that score.

CHRISTINE: All right then—suppose that, in addition to not caring about being a hypocrite, they didn't care about hurting others.

BEN: You may be describing a sociopath. Insofar as this person is not in a socially powerful position, it will still be rational for him to publicly endorse the moral system, since it will offer him protections against stronger persons, including other sociopaths who might be wilier, more violently inclined, or better armed. But given his interests, values, and attitudes, it may well be that no good argument could be provided to him for going beyond public endorsement and agreeing to comply with the moral system in his actual behavior.

CHRISTINE: But that seems to mean it's OK for them to be a sociopath!

BEN: No. Maybe some sadistic person who doesn't care about what others think of him enjoys hurting others emotionally or physically. So he does, when he thinks he can get away with it. But he's acting immorally, because he's violating the moral rules. The fact that he doesn't care, or that he even likes doing what he's doing, provides no moral justification for his actions.

But even this person, assuming that he does not have some powerful position in society that makes him immune to threats, is still rationally required to publicly endorse the moral system. That's a powerful result. What we probably can't get, given his specific personality and values, is an argument that is a good one for him to the effect that he should also agree to live by the moral standards he has publicly endorsed.

SHARIFA: What if a person just doesn't face up to his own hypocrisy? Really, he hates the idea of himself as a hypocrite, but he still says no to the idea of living according to the moral system. He doesn't accept the argument to do so because he just puts out of mind the hypocrisy of his intention to act immorally even though he has publicly endorsed the moral system.

BEN: Such a person is simply not facing up to the fact that his own values provide a good argument for complying with the moral system. He's engaged in self-deception. There will always be those who refuse to follow an argument where it naturally leads. But what we're interested in is the conclusions deliberators *should* come to given their worldviews and values, not in some blind or defensive refusal to acknowledge what those beliefs and values entail.

CHARLIE: The contrast to all this hypocrisy would be someone like Nietzsche, who was quite up front talking about what he didn't like about morality.

BEN: Nietzsche is a refreshing exception to common hypocrisy about morality. In *On the Genealogy of Morality*, he is pretty explicit that conventional morality is a degenerate system. In his story, a religion like Christianity, with its emphasis in the New Testament on turning the other cheek, charity, the valorization of the meek, and the suspicion of the wealthy, is a case study of the weak finding ideological solace in a supposedly moral system that is really, according to Nietzsche, just formalized resentment. It's a vendetta by the helpless and incompetent against the strong and competent. He saw Christianity as a reaction against the age of the Greek heroes—great-souled men who accomplished great deeds with great courage and who, in the process, showed no pity toward any lesser men whose lives might be harmed or even destroyed as they heroically carry out their projects. It was the resentment of the weak against these great spirits that gave rise to Christianity—a morality for slaves, in Nietzsche's estimation.

Nietzsche's ideal of the *Übermensch* or over-man is modeled on the Greek heroes, or his glorifying conception of them. He saw a worthwhile life as one that cast off the limitations and sense of guilt embedded in conventional morality in favor of a project of self-creation.

CHARLIE: I love Nietzsche. But I can see now that this is a sort of ethical egoism that could never be rationally endorsed by the deliberative committee.

MATT: I hate Nietzsche probably at least as much as you love him. What can the attraction be? You can't be saying that it's OK for some person in full self-creation mode to trample over the rights of others. It's so elitist and arrogant!

CHARLIE: I see what you mean. What's clear to me now is that you can't take what Nietzsche seems to suggest in the *Genealogy* and elsewhere seriously as a set of general guidelines for how a society should be structured. It really isn't acceptable to hurt other people in the pursuit of your own happiness without regard to their rights, including their rights to pursue their own self-creation projects. But if you reject the part of Nietzsche that seems to justify any harm done to others if your self-creation project is brilliant enough, you do get an intriguing idea in support of people living creatively. There's a lot to be said for celebrating non-conformity and for rethinking all the routines and conventional ideas in a society.

BEN: I think Nietzsche is an important philosopher to read because he's very good at one of the main tasks of a philosopher. He looks critically at some of our most sacrosanct ideas and practices. That doesn't mean, of course, that you have to agree with him. It seems to me that, applying the philosopher's critical thinking tools to Nietzsche himself, you'll find, along with some real insights, a lot to disagree with—certainly including those passages suggesting that self-creation projects can override conventional morality. But Nietzsche himself would have to approve of that examination.

Earlier I mentioned moral nihilism as a wholesale rejection of morality. It's the denial that there are any moral truths. Nietzsche holds some strongly affirmative views about human life and the possibility of progress, so I don't think it would be fair to classify him as a nihilist through and through. But he does seem to be endorsing *moral* nihilism with his claim that morality is a false ideology perpetrated by those whose interest this ideology serves.

Even though he focuses his attack on what he calls Christian moral-ity, it's pretty clear that he's critical of principles and guidelines that any moral point of view would endorse. It seems equally clear, though, that deliberators would reject a society structured around Nietzschean or other moral nihilist ideas. A society that took as its governing idea that morality was a sham to be accorded no respect would be one that countenanced no moral teaching, no punish-ments for behavior that we would—falsely, the nihilists would say—consider to be immoral, and so on. It would in effect be a society with no system for regulating behavior at all—an anarchic society that even the nihilists, on reflection, would see they could not ratio-nally endorse, were they to find themselves on Professor Ishida's deliberative committee.

CHRISTINE: What about Sartre and the other Existentialists? Aren't they similar to Nietzsche in rejecting conventional morality?

BEN: Not explicitly, nor was it their intent, as I read them. It may be that some readers of the Existentialists use their ideas as an excuse for immorality or for not taking morality seriously. But I don't think any of the Existentialists themselves would endorse such immoral-ism. It's true that Sartre's concern with the value of living in good faith—authentically—is very much in line with Nietzsche's ideal of freely creating oneself. But as Charlie has already noted, you can take self-creation as a valuable idea and a worthwhile goal to pursue while still understanding that it has to be pursued within the context of the moral system. You don't get to find your authentic self if doing so unjustifiably harms someone else or deprives them of their freedom to engage in their own projects.

CHRISTINE: Didn't Sartre say, "Hell is other people"?

BEN: He has a character in one of his plays say that, but I don't think it meant "*To* hell with other people!" Maybe he was making a point about how we can get trapped by others' definitions of who we are. In any case, Sartre's obvious concern with our ethical obligations, for example, in the case he famously described of a young man trying to decide whether his strongest obligation is to stay home and care for his mother or to join the resistance against the Nazis, indicates a strong respect for morality. In his later work, he was concerned about social justice.

CHARLIE: Even if I'm recognizing the validity of the moral system and agreeing to comply with it, isn't it clear that these ideals of personal freedom that you find in philosophers like Nietzsche and Sartre are more important values than, say, acting to help others? Given that I'm not violating others' rights, I don't see that I should have to go out of my way to help them when I've got my own projects that are valuable to me.

BEN: Different specific moral systems are going to disagree about this. Some approaches to Utilitarianism, for example, suggest that you do have overriding obligations to help others if that produces more good for others than harm to yourself. Gert thinks that there are legitimate differences in the degree to which people can value personal freedom compared to aiding others less well off. So it's one of those areas where he thinks there's no one right way to balance these competing values. There are also relevant empirical questions that need to be taken into account in resolving—if we can—some of these debates. In any case, these are debates that would need to be further discussed in ordinary social contexts. It's not within the deliberative committee's charge to resolve questions at this level of detail. So you'll just have to make your case for the greater value of personal freedom in further discussions within whatever society the deliberators choose.

# The Deliberative Committee
# and Relativism

BEN: Christine, you've been defending moral relativism. What are your thoughts about this as you imagine yourself making your decisions on the deliberative committee?

CHRISTINE: Well, I've seen some difficulties with moral relativism when we were discussing it earlier. But I'd like to think more about this, so why don't I approach it with the full-throated relativistic beliefs that I started with and see how that goes.

BEN: Sure.

CHRISTINE: But I'm not sure I know exactly what I'm deliberating about in this case. I know that relativism is in opposition to the moral system because it doesn't accept that there's one system of morality that applies universally to all cultures and all moral agents. And as deliberators, we're supposed to decide which of these we could rationally endorse. You've given us a pretty clear picture of what the moral system is and what it would be like to live under it. But I guess I'm not sure just what a society that embraced moral relativism would look like.

BEN: There are actually different versions of moral relativism. Sometimes relativists focus on a society or culture, with the idea that different cultures have different moralities. That's what we're calling cultural relativism—the idea that an act is morally right if and only if it's approved of in the culture where it takes place. Others focus on the individual and say that morality is relative to each person—what's moral is just whatever a given individual sincerely believes is moral. But I think it's clear that that sort of subjective relativism is not going to fare very well with the deliberative committee. Even if the committee includes someone initially sympathetic to subjective relativism, it's not going to be rational for others to accept a system in which every individual's belief in what's morally right by their own lights is accepted without any societal constraints. It's not rational to put no constraints on the sociopath or the child molester.

MATT: I think that sort of subjective relativism is going to fare just the same among deliberators as ethical egoism or moral nihilism.

CHRISTINE: That sounds right. I think my real interest has been cultural relativism. What I'm concerned about is when one culture thinks it can impose its values, as supposedly universal values, on every other culture. And when Professor Ishida defends the moral system as universal, it sounds too much like just that sort of imposition. So it makes me look toward the idea that, instead of some one universal moral system, we have a plurality of different moral worlds, each one relative to a particular culture. But I'm not clear what that idea comes to as a system to be compared to the moral system.

BEN: I think most people who espouse moral relativism are like you in having something more like cultural relativism in mind, rather than subjective relativism. But it's often held as a rather vague idea. That may be why it's hard to figure out exactly what kind of system the deliberators would be reflecting on when deciding whether they could rationally endorse cultural relativism. One problem is how to define what constitutes a society or culture. A Mob boss belongs to a culture in which it's OK to have hit men rub out the rival, but maybe he also belongs to the Catholic Church as well as being a U.S. citizen. While Catholic and U.S. cultural norms agree in their disapproval of Mafia-ordered killing, they disagree between themselves about other practices, for example, concerning divorce and capital punishment. So which culture does the Mob boss's action get evaluated by? If a person can belong to more than one culture, and those cultures have conflicting rules about what behavior is acceptable, rewarded, and punished, then cultural relativism is incoherent in terms of offering guidelines about what the person should do.

CHRISTINE: Why don't we define a culture in terms of national boundaries, at least for the sake of argument?

BEN: OK. The idea then would be that if the deliberators chose this system, they would be choosing to live, and have everyone live, in a system in which nations are the ultimate arbiter of what behavior gets rewarded, allowed, and punished, both formally and informally.

CHRISTINE: Meaning, if I live in the U.S. then all the norms in U.S. society—not just the formal laws but the informal norms regarding how people treat each other—are correct for those living in that society, including me? I'm already realizing a difficulty here because there are a lot of our culture's norms that I'm critical of. I guess I don't get to pick and choose the norms I like, do I?

BEN: No, because it's the culture, not the individual, that defines what's morally right and wrong. I suppose you could tinker with the definition of what a culture is—trying out something besides nation-states as the determinant of what counts as a culture—but you're likely to get the same results in terms of what deliberators could rationally endorse.

CHRISTINE: Yeah, I see that. And I see that accepting cultural relativism does create tensions with other things I believe. But I still want to follow through with this idea of cultural relativism and see specifically if Professor Ishida is right that it can't pass muster with the deliberative committee. I'm getting the sense that relativism doesn't work, but I also want to see if her method explains *why* it doesn't work. So let me just accept cultural relativism as we've defined it, with U.S. values being the morally correct ones in the U.S. but not necessarily elsewhere. At least then we can say that other cultures outside our own are self-determining. We can't insist that we have all the moral authority and demand that those other cultures adopt our values. I still like that idea.

SHARIFA: So assuming this sort of relativism is true, are we as deliberators accepting everything in the U.S. as it is right now?

BEN: The existing norms of a society are by definition correct.

SHARIFA: OK. And the criteria for deliberators to make a decision include whether all deliberators could rationally endorse the system under discussion. But I couldn't rationally endorse this cultural relativist system.

CHRISTINE: Why not?

SHARIFA: Because while this country is a pretty decent one, especially when you compare it to a lot of other countries, it's not where it ought to be in all things.

CHRISTINE: Well, no country is perfect, not even the hypothetical society that operates as best it can within the parameters of the moral system as we are imagining that society.

SHARIFA: Right, but I'm thinking of an existing negative ste-reotype about Muslims in present-day U.S. culture. Since 9/11 there have been a lot of unreasonable attitudes and outright discrimination and even violence toward ordinary Muslim Americans. I'm not say-ing it's pervasive or that I'd rather live in Egypt or another Muslim country. I wouldn't. I love it here. It's my country, and I do appreci-ate the American ideal of a society that is open to and tolerant of all religious and ethnic groups. But it's an ideal that, over a lot of our country's history and into the present, hasn't always been put into practice. Cultural relativism says that there's no moral problem with existing negative attitudes and discrimination toward Muslims to the extent that they actually exist. My choice as a deliberator is between the moral system, which strives to treat every moral agent fairly no matter what their ethnic or religious background is, and this cultural relativist system, which says that whatever current norms and attitudes exist are morally right. But as a Muslim it would be irrational for me to accept that relativist system—it puts people of my faith at risk of unjust treatment and harms for no compensating gain for us.

CHRISTINE: But is this discriminatory attitude part of the norm of our society? It's not a good thing when it happens, but I believe we have laws now against this sort of discrimination. So our social norms are against this sort of unfair treatment, even if some individu-als violate those norms.

BEN: I don't think you can get relativism off the hook quite that easily, Christine. Remember that the systems that we're comparing include more than just the formal laws of a society. They also include general tendencies regarding how people treat each other in everyday contexts. There can be laws on the books prohibiting discrimination against those of minority races, ethnicities, and religions, but these laws may be widely ignored, with little or no attempt to enforce them. If so, then cultural relativism in effect endorses that disregard of the laws and lack of enforcement within that society.

SHARIFA: So in a society under the moral system, by contrast, there would be an attempt to correct these sorts of discriminatory norms, right?

BEN: Yes, because, thinking in terms of Gert's system, the dis-criminations unjustifiably violate one or more of the moral rules. Just think of the moral rules "Do not cause pain" and "Do not deprive of freedom." Pain can include emotional as well as physical pain. When ethnic or religious groups are discriminated against—when someone can't get a job or a good home, a child is teased in school, and so on—this not only deprives people of freedom but creates significant emotional pain. A morally just society is concerned about recognizing such injustices and working to rectify them.

CHRISTINE: OK. I think I see why it's not going to be rational for deliberators like Sharifa to endorse the cultural relativist system. But just for the sake of argument, I have a couple more questions. Cultural relativism accepts the existing norms of a society as they are, but in the case of U.S. society, isn't the idea of moral improvement sort of built into our social code? Ben and Sharifa have both acknowledged that there's been moral progress in our society.

I totally agree that there's a problem regarding current attitudes toward Muslims—and others too. We're still not where we should be in terms of existing problems of racism and sexism, for example. But I think that, given our country's history, there's good reason to think that we will further progress as a society. There was unfair discrimination against ordinary Japanese Americans during World War II. Our country deprived them of their property and confined them to internment camps for years. Remember Professor Ishida telling us that both her parents were in these camps as children? This was our country's unreasonable and unfair reaction during wartime. But that anti-Japanese attitude has dissipated. We now see it for the fearful and ethnocentric attitude that it in fact was—and I think the anti-Muslim attitude will dissipate too in time.

MATT: But we don't know that society will change. Sometimes we do progress, but sometimes we regress too. There aren't guarantees. The problem with cultural relativism is that it locks in, as morally acceptable, whatever norms currently exist in the society, including discrimination, if that's a feature of the way people treat some groups in that society.

BEN: That's right. And because most actual societies typically have a number of norms and beliefs that are in some tension with each other, what you get with cultural relativism is a hodgepodge of norms, some that common morality tells us are morally good, like some of our society's ideals of equality and the possibility of progress, but also some that common morality tells us are morally wrong, like discrimination. The problem is that cultural relativism puts these very different tendencies and attitudes on a par.

MATT: And here's another problem that I think is even more serious: There are a lot of moral flaws in our society. But we also have in place a lot of positive values favoring freedom, equality, and so on. To a lot of people, U.S. values and practices can look, overall, like a pretty good deal. But we're imagining that deliberators can come from any society, right? Not just ours?

BEN: Not only can they, they must. To really understand Professor Ishida's thought experiment, we have to imagine not just us as deliberators but any moral agent. Not just ourselves in our society, and not just other moral agents in other contemporary societies, but those living in past societies as well.

MATT: But that does clinch the case against cultural relativism, doesn't it? There are still societies today—not just in the past—with norms that allow punishing or even killing someone just because of their religion or their ethnicity. It would be irrational for a deliberator in a generally very oppressive society, or in a society that severely discriminates against members of his race or religion, to endorse the cultural relativist moral system. Such a system simply accepts as moral all that oppression and violence. By contrast, it *would* be rational for them to endorse the moral system, which would discourage and punish such oppressive behavior.

BEN: I think that does clinch the case. But then, I'm not the one that needs convincing. Christine?

CHRISTINE: Yeah, I agree. I was pretty much already there coming into today's discussion, given previous conversations. It's pretty clear that cultural relativism isn't right and isn't the theory I was looking for. I think my concern, coming into this course, was with the way our society in particular tends to think it's so superior to all the others. I have to agree that it's a lot better than it used to be in its treatment of African Americans and women, for example. But even with those improvements, I think there have been, throughout its history and very much into the present, too many times when our mainstream culture fails to understand values and practices that aren't part of the mainstream. And that lack of understanding leads to elitism and intolerance. But I see now that my criticism of our culture itself relies on moral values, and I can't say those values are just personal to me, or else my criticism couldn't really have the extent and force that I think it should have.

I was really affected by our discussion of tolerance early in the semester, before you came into our discussions, Ben. That helped me see that it was really my valuing of tolerance that was a key factor in my dislike of the ways U.S. and Western culture have exerted unjust dominance over others. I saw that if I were really a relativist, I wouldn't be able to claim that there was some sort of global injustice in these cultural practices. Cultural relativism doesn't allow us to criticize any one culture's moral beliefs, but I do want to criticize U.S. culture when it is arrogant—and also, I see now, Japanese culture or any other culture when *it's* been arrogant. My own values aren't consistent with saying a culture's practices are always right.

Our earlier discussion also helped me see that there are limits to tolerance as well: that I don't want to tolerate intolerance and that I do, by my own lights, want to morally criticize intolerant societies—*any* such society, not just mine.

BEN: So you recognize that cultural relativism isn't your theory after all. Is it then the moral system? Or would that still be irrational for you to endorse?

CHRISTINE: I want to know what Professor Ishida meant when she said you could have this universal and objective morality even though it doesn't provide a definitive answer about what's right or wrong in every case. I'm not sure how this is supposed to work. Another thing that had attracted me to relativism was that I assumed that believing in a universal and objective moral system meant believing in these definitive answers. And I just didn't see how there could be a clear-cut answer all the time. I'm more attracted to some version of moral objectivism if it does accept that there's not always one and only one right answer.

BEN: Your background assumption is understandable. Many moral theorists do take the position that you can get a definitive answer about an action's morality in every case. But this isn't a position that follows from the very idea of objective morality. From the fact that there's no objectively correct answer in *some* cases, it doesn't follow that there's no such answer in *all* cases. Consider a genocide instigated by some power-hungry demagogue manipulating one ethnic group's enmity toward another. This is a pretty clear case of an objectively wrong set of actions. And, from even one such definitive example, it follows that objective moral facts do exist.

Even when there may be no determinate resolution regarding what the morally *right* course of action is, there can still be many objectively *wrong* ways of resolving it. Here's a useful analogy from Bernard Gert: Consider the question, "Who's the best baseball player of all time?" There may not be one objectively correct answer to that question, no matter how much statistical analysis one does. There are too many acceptably different ways to weigh all the different factors that count toward excellence in baseball. But the fact that there's no one right answer doesn't mean that there aren't a lot of wrong answers. Need a wrong answer? Just name any player who had an undistinguished record for a couple years on a lousy team before he was unceremoniously shown the door. Similarly, you can still talk about clearly morally wrong approaches to a moral dilemma even when there are some unresolvable debates about the right approach.

CHRISTINE: So some specific dilemma like whether my boyfriend should blow the whistle on his boss might not have one right answer?

BEN: That could be the case. Often one has to look at the specific details, including morally relevant circumstances that make up the factual background, to make a judgment about particular cases.

MATT: Doesn't this make almost everything morally unresolved?

BEN: Less than you'd think. Christine is probably right that one of the factors that has made cultural relativism, or even subjective relativism, appealing to a lot of people is the perception that there is so much moral disagreement among societies and among individuals. But at least some of that disagreement is not disagreement about morality at all—it's disagreement about the *non*-moral facts on the ground or about the proper way to describe the situation in question. For example, people debating capital punishment may disagree about factual matters such as whether it is an effective deterrent. Debates about the legalization and use of drugs are often largely driven by differing beliefs about non-moral facts concerning the nature and extent of addictive properties in various drugs, whether making particular drugs illegal has better social consequences than allowing them to be legal, and so on. There often does remain a core of moral disagreement, but the gap between people regarding their purely moral beliefs is typically not as wide as it can seem.

MATT: But regarding that "core of moral disagreement," it seems like some of the most important debates of our time, like abortion, are going to be unresolved. That's pretty unsatisfying.

BEN: Gert would probably agree that it's unsatisfying. But he thinks that philosophers distort the moral system when they try to make it fit into an either/or model, where every last action can be categorized clearly as morally acceptable or morally unacceptable.

It's an interesting and open question just how extensive such morally unresolvable debates are. Gert thinks that there are unresolvable moral disagreements about how much freedom it is appropriate to sacrifice in order to accommodate entities like human fetuses and animals that lack moral agency. Professor Ishida is more optimistic, even about such notable controversies as abortion and animal rights. She isn't convinced that the extent of indeterminacy is as great as Gert believes. She thinks that there are considerations outside of morality proper—not just scientific or other ordinary factual considerations but metaphysical arguments too—that can be brought to bear to create reasonable arguments in favor of some of these positions over others. But that's a question for another day, not something Professor Ishida's deliberative committee has to grapple with.

There is one point regarding the extent and scope of morally unresolvable debates that Gert and Professor Ishida agree about and think can't be emphasized enough. They believe that the big moral debates that are so prominent in society give us a misleading picture. These debates suggest that moral disagreement is widespread and based on fundamentally different and irreconcilable moral worldviews. This picture is misleading because it keeps us from noticing how widespread moral *agreement* among people really is.

CHRISTINE: Where do they find widespread agreement?

BEN: Well, when you think about the fact that every human being is performing actions of some kind or another throughout almost every waking moment of their lives, it seems clear that there really isn't much if any controversy about upwards of 99 percent of those actions—the acts of preparing dinner, or saying a kind word to a neighbor, or reading bedtime stories to your children are not regarded as anything but morally acceptable. And there are a lot of ordinary, or extraordinary, crimes and other actions of individuals or cultures that aren't very controversially assessed as morally wrong. We tend to forget about such areas of widespread agreement because we, quite understandably, focus on the problem cases.

MATT: But of course there *are* real controversies. I can think of lots of actions of cultures and governments in particular where people disagree about the moral assessment.

BEN: Right. But especially at the level of actions taken by a government or other cultural entity, it's hard to assess the often enormously complex but morally relevant factual circumstances and background, such as the perceptions and intentions of the main players, the short- and long-term consequences, and so on. So the disagreement may still be primarily about the empirical facts surrounding the case, not about morality in and of itself.

But you're right. It's pretty clear that some moral debates are genuinely intractable. If the approach Gert and Professor Ishida take to these questions is right, then, as in many other cases, the reality is not as ideal as the optimists would have it but not as bleak as the pessimists take it to be.

# The Deliberative Committee on Animal Rights and Racism

CHRISTINE: So I've been thinking about this idea of morally unresolvable disagreements. On the one hand, I'm glad that the moral system doesn't necessarily offer an absolute yes/no right/wrong answer about every question. I had thought only relativism could be like that. On the other hand, I want some of these disagreements to be resolved! I'm particularly concerned about how in this society we kill animals for food and kill or hurt them in experiments, when the usefulness of those experiments is often highly questionable.

BEN: So you think meat eating is morally wrong?

CHRISTINE: Yes.

BEN: And not just for yourself?

CHRISTINE: Right. It's not just a personal preference. I think the unnecessary suffering we cause animals is unconscionable.

BEN: Let's discuss that, but first I have to point out that this is another way in which you can't really consistently be a moral relativist. You are making a moral judgment that makes reference to the objective wrongness of animal suffering.

MATT: So do you really think it's objectively wrong in that sense, Christine?

CHRISTINE: I think that if people can get their nutritional needs met without meat, then it's wrong for them to eat it. And in our society almost everyone can meet their nutritional needs without meat. So yes, I think it's wrong.

CHARLIE: And that's not just a judgment relative to our society?

CHRISTINE: Before, I would have said it's just relative to our society. But I see now that cultural relativism can't really support things I care about. What's moral or immoral can depend on circumstances, as Ben has been pointing out. But it's not plausible to think that the sole circumstance determining morality is the norms of the society that the action happens to take place in. In fact, I still think that meat eating can be morally acceptable in some societies. But that's not because culture determines morality. It's because in that particular society it might be hard to easily get adequate nutrition without meat. In traditional Inuit culture, they couldn't plant vegetable gardens in the ice and snow. They pretty much had to rely on their catches of fish, seals, and whales. And there might be individuals with medical conditions that would make it risky for them not to have some meat in their diet. But these are exceptions. Most of us these days don't need meat and so we shouldn't eat it. Period.

BEN: A lot of people who are initially attracted to cultural relativism find that they actually have a lot of pretty strong moral beliefs that are in fact incompatible with relativism. Sounds like that's happened to you.

CHRISTINE: That's right. I'm getting off that boat and it can float away without me!

So if I'm not going to go along with relativism, I have some attraction to endorsing the moral system, but my feelings about animal rights make me wonder if it would really be rational for me to endorse it. Sharifa says that it would be irrational for her to endorse the cultural relativist system, because it would allow currently discriminatory attitudes toward Muslims to persist that risk harming her for no compensating gain. And I accept her point. But what about my own aversion to a society where tens of millions of animals are unnecessarily killed and eaten? Sharifa can stand up for herself and argue rightly against discrimination. But animals can't advocate for themselves. I feel like it's up to people like me to do that. It would be irrational for a parent to endorse a system that said that since babies and toddlers aren't moral agents, it's OK to kill them. Even though young children aren't moral agents, parents would be deeply harmed emotionally by a system that allowed their children to be abused or enslaved or killed. So why can't I say that it's irrational for me to endorse a system that allows animals to be abused and killed, given that I'm concerned about their suffering? Also, given my values, I see no compensating gain in a society in which they are killed and eaten.

CHARLIE: So you would equate animals to people?

CHRISTINE: No. I recognize the greater value of a human life. If I had to choose between a chicken dying and a human, of course I'd choose the chicken. Human lives are richer and more complex and meaningful. But that doesn't mean a chicken, or a cow or a pig, has *no* value. And since we *don't* have to choose between these animals' lives and humans' lives, at least regarding our decisions about what to put in our supermarket carts, we should respect that value.

BEN: One difference is that all rational adult humans are moral agents. Under the moral system, all moral agents come under the full protection of the principles of morality. No moral agent could rationally allow himself to be excluded from that protection. But non-moral agents can't be part of the deliberative process, so it remains an open question how much, if any, protection they should receive. It's not that your moral vegetarianism is wrong. It's just that our deliberative scenario can't produce a rational requirement that all deliberators should extend full protection of the moral principles to animals or to some subset of "higher" animals.

CHRISTINE: But toddlers aren't moral agents either. As we've discussed, it isn't very controversial that it's morally wrong to kill toddlers. Why is it controversial that it's wrong to kill animals?

BEN: At least in part because toddlers will become moral agents. And it's moral agency that has a lot to do with the richer and more complex lives of humans that make their lives more valuable than the lives of animals, as you've acknowledged.

CHRISTINE: I understand that the level of concern might be more intense when it's parent–child versus human–animal. But that's just a matter of degree.

BEN: I don't think it is just a matter of degree. A chicken is not going to become a moral agent, but a toddler will. So we're talking about what appear to be morally significant differences in the kinds of entities they are, not just about degrees of attachment or concern.

CHRISTINE: Well, as long as we remember that animals can experience physical pain much as we experience it, I'll grant that there are intellectual and emotional capacities humans have that make them qualitatively different from animals in some ways. But I'm not clear how this point relates to whether moral vegetarians like me can rationally endorse the moral system.

BEN: Keep in mind that in endorsing it within Professor Ishida's deliberative context, you are not endorsing meat eating. You are deliberating on a broadly moral framework that leaves unaddressed many specific moral debates. So you wouldn't be endorsing a system that allows animals to be killed. You would be endorsing a system that doesn't take any particular stand on that.

And it isn't really accurate to say that there would be no compensating gains for you, given your values, if you endorsed the moral system. In addition to the general benefits that come to you from endorsing it—as we've seen, it protects you, in a way that ethical egoism does not, from strong individuals who pursue only their self-interest—the moral system seems to me the best system for you to make your case for moral vegetarianism. Cultural relativism won't support across-the-board respect for animal rights—few if any cultures have in place the norms for protecting animals that you would like to see. Ethical egoism would leave everything to the self-interests of individual humans. So it's very unlikely that this system would result in greater respect for animals. And a religious system may or may not include respect for animals among its teachings.

CHRISTINE: OK. I agree that it would be rational for me to endorse the moral system if I'm not thereby endorsing meat eating and if the deliberative committee couldn't rationally agree to accept moral vegetarianism. But I don't see why they couldn't agree to it.

BEN: Other moral agents can't be rationally required to endorse moral vegetarianism within the parameters of what is up for debate in Professor Ishida's particular deliberative context. You'll get agreement among deliberators regarding toddlers. Deliberators could not rationally accept a system in which it was the norm to kill or harm young children. But you won't get such agreement regarding the treatment of animals. In terms of Gert's moral rules, deliberators would not all rationally agree to the extension of such rules as "do not cause pain, do not kill" to animals. This would require many deliberators to sacrifice significant freedom to eat as they've been accustomed to eating, to enjoy the variety a meat diet introduces to one's palette, to eat foods that have a culturally significant role in holiday meals, and so on. But *within* the moral system, if that's the general framework that you and the other deliberators agree to, you might be able to construct a compelling argument, in the sense we discussed of a reasonable argument that others *ought* to accept, in favor of moral vegetarianism. You could appeal, for example, to empirical facts about animals' capacity to feel pain, to factory farm conditions, and so on, and you could make the case that values such as enjoying the taste of meat should not trump values of respect for the lives of animals. You could use such points to try to show that these considerations ought to trump practical considerations of convenience or cost or theological claims about humans' relations to animals.

CHRISTINE: Especially if theological claims come into play, I'm not sure I could convince anyone.

BEN: Remember that the question isn't whether your arguments would actually change some particular individual's mind, but whether they are good arguments for that person that she ought to accept. Religious texts often leave room for interpretation such that evidence we've recently acquired about animals' lives and capabilities might make it reasonable to believe that these texts should be interpreted in a way favorable to animal rights.

Of course, the openness to compelling arguments works both ways. Others might present good arguments that might successfully respond to your arguments for moral vegetarianism. You'd have to keep an open mind about that.

These would all be debates that would take place outside the deliberative context in whatever society the deliberative committee agreed to endorse. But if the moral system is endorsed, the society thus endorsed will be disposed to adopt the policies that the strongest arguments point to as those that best exemplify moral behavior.

CHARLIE: What about the debate about moral agency itself? On the deliberative committee, everyone can bring their actual beliefs and values to the table. And there have been and continue to be views out there that some adult humans are not moral agents because they are of another race, ethnicity, or religion—that in fact they are subhuman. I'm not suggesting anything like that is true, of course. But why couldn't some white racist argue that it's irrational for him to limit his own freedoms in order to extend protection of the moral rules to black people? He would argue against such protection, since in his view they are not fully deserving of the moral status and protections accorded to white people. Is it that such beliefs are false—is that why a racist couldn't use them?

BEN: Unfortunately, no. Deliberators are allowed to bring all their existing beliefs to the table. And a lot of them, not just these racist beliefs, have to be false. You'll have theists and atheists coming together to choose a common system. If the theists' beliefs about the existence of a deity are true, then the atheists' beliefs are false and vice versa. So we can't exclude a belief just because it's false.

CHARLIE: Then what's to prevent the racist from saying that it's irrational for him to endorse the moral system because treating those of another race as equals limits his freedom and provides him with no compensating gains given his values?

BEN: The first thing to note is that the racist will never get the deliberative committee to publicly endorse his views. It would be irrational for others—first and foremost those of the race he opposes—to endorse such views.

CHARLIE: Sure. But then why don't we have an impasse, where nothing gets resolved? Why would it be rational for the racist to endorse the moral system?

BEN: By the rules for deliberation, the racist has to endorse what the others are all agreeing to endorse, unless it's irrational for him to do so. *If* the racist's beliefs are deeply embedded into his worldview, then it might indeed be the case that it would be irrational for him to publicly endorse the moral system. But it's worth thinking about how often this would occur. One important feature of Professor Ishida's deliberative structure to note in this context is that the deliberative process itself would lead a lot of racists to recognize the moral agency of fellow deliberators. Many individuals who live in racist societies and who belong to the dominating race just go along with a system that gives them advantages and privileges. They are still racists, for sure, because they are participating in and implicitly accepting a racist system and the advantages they gain from it. But they may not be deeply committed to an ideology that denies moral agency and basic rights to those of the other race. So consider what happens when such racists of this free rider sort are put on the level playing field of the deliberative committee. They experience those of the other race as fellow deliberators. It seems pretty clear that such racists typically won't be able to reasonably sustain a belief to the effect that their fellow deliberator lacks moral agency or has no right to equal treatment under the principles of morality on the grounds that he is of another race. He will see the moral agency of that person in action!

CHARLIE: What about someone whose racism goes deeper?

BEN: Even regarding a more ideologically committed racist, a lot of the hatred and the false racial beliefs they've acquired come about because they have been indoctrinated with a picture of the vileness of members of the other race. This picture is often sustained by segregation and by power-imbalanced interactions in their daily lives. The falsity of this picture becomes pretty manifest when the racist has to try to defend his racism in the presence of his deliberative peers as they work to define a society all can rationally endorse.

Keep in mind, too, that in order for it to be irrational for the racist to endorse the moral system, he can't just believe that he will lose benefits under it. He would have to believe that he would be subject to serious harms with no compensating gain. The reasonable belief is that I am not harmed, indeed am likely benefited, by allowing to other humans the sort of freedom I enjoy. Of course, there's no guarantee that a strong racist will have, or arrive at, such a reasonable belief. But they would have to sustain, throughout the deliberative process and in conversation with someone who is in fact a moral agent, a belief that this person and others of his race are not moral agents and that it would be a significant harm to himself to allow them the freedom of being protected by the moral rules. He would also have to keep in mind that, in a society under the moral system, he too is protected by the moral rules from any racist attitudes or beliefs toward his own race. I think most racists would find it hard, when engaging with a deliberator of the other race, to reasonably sustain the racist beliefs they began with.

CHARLIE: But this is still an empirical question. You think many or most actual racists would change their beliefs in the deliberative setting. But how do we really know?

BEN: There are empirical aspects to this, for sure. But remember that we are looking at the quality of the arguments the racist would bring to the table. A given racist might retain such a strong psychological aversion to those of the other race that he would be unwilling to accept the good arguments made available to him in the deliberative context. It certainly bears thinking about further, but it may well be that the *only* explanation for racist deliberators' continued unwillingness to endorse morality would be this sort of psychological obstinacy. Given the evidence they have that there is no compelling reason for this aversion, they don't have good reason for their racist beliefs, and they do have good reason to endorse morality. So the simple refusal of a deliberator to accept arguments that are good arguments for him does not count as a case of a reasonable rejection of the moral system.

I hope it's clear that everything I've said here about the racist applies to someone who has this attitude toward those of a different ethnicity—it's not that the difference is specifically racial that matters. It also applies to sexist attitudes treating someone unfairly on account of gender.

# The Deliberative Committee and Religion

BEN: So moral relativism and—earlier—ethical egoism have been tried and found wanting—to say nothing of even more extreme views like racism and moral nihilism.

But what about religion? What's its relation to morality, and what would the deliberators say about adopting a religious system of guidelines as opposed to the moral system?

SHARIFA: Right. I now see that this question has to come up. When you introduced the moral system, Matt expressed dismay that you would separate religion out from morality as something that could be opposed to morality. Like Matt, I was perplexed at that point. But I see now what you were saying.

I was glad to hear you agree with Matt that for the most part religion upholds morality and indeed that, without religion, the practice of morality, to the extent that we humans have achieved it, perhaps would never have become established. But I understand now that religion claims a good deal more than what morality, taken by itself, is concerned with. I see that religions incorporate teachings that go beyond morality in revealing Allah or some other deity as the creator of the world. We embed the idea of moral goodness in that deity and think of him as providing a sense of love and meaning in the universe. So to me, and I'm sure to Matt too, religion both explains morality and gives us a richer and truer picture of the world than morality can by itself. But I also have to agree with you that sometimes religious practice and teaching can go astray morally. You mentioned the Spanish Inquisition as an example of immorality undertaken in the name of religion. Perhaps you were too polite to mention people who have acted immorally in the name of my faith. The 9/11 terrorists claimed to be acting in the name of Islam, but what they did was hideous and evil. It's not anything like Islam as I was taught it and as I know it to be.

MATT: But when religious institutions, or sects within them, go off the rails like that, isn't that *always* outside the real spirit of the religion? Aren't the core teachings of religion about the moral life?

BEN: Well, as Sharifa's remarks suggest, most religions would probably say their core teachings are about God and humans' relations to God as that religion conceives these things. And as we've seen, those aren't in fact questions of morality proper. Whether God exists and what his nature is are questions of theology and metaphysics rather than morality.

SHARIFA: Some people do say that all religions are ultimately saying the same thing in terms of their core teachings.

CHARLIE: But that's not literally true when it comes to things like whether you have to believe in Jesus in order to be saved.

SHARIFA: Agreed—that's a real difference. We noted earlier how Islam regards Jesus as a great teacher but as only a human being. And of course many Hindus may not even have heard of Jesus or Mohammed, or even God. But isn't there still something universal in all the different religions' messages of peace, justice, forgiveness, compassion, and love?

BEN: That may well be. But I think it's significant that when you describe these universal beliefs, they really amount to dropping the specifically theological and religious teachings and reasserting the common moral sentiments of humanity.

CHARLIE: So let's think about a religious system with its distinctly religious teachings and doctrines as a competitor to the moral system. What I'm thinking of is the Ten Commandments as given in the Bible. We've seen how the deliberators would reject as irrational other systems. Now suppose the Ten Commandments were the governing rules of the society instead of something like Gert's ten moral rules. It seems to me that the religious rules couldn't pass muster in the deliberative committee.

MATT: So what is it specifically about the Ten Commandments that's the problem? Some of those commands are the same as Gert's moral rules—like "Do not kill" and "Do not bear false witness," which essentially means don't lie or deceive.

CHARLIE: Right. But consider the rule to set aside one day of the week and keep it holy. Typically that has meant don't work, spend time in church, and so on. And this is presented as a command from God, not something you can take or leave. But it would be irrational for *me* to accept a system that required me to go to church to worship a God I don't believe in or care about. As an atheist, I'm certainly going to feel like I have better things to do with my time than go to church.

MATT: But these may not be the key ideas of Christianity. In any case, these days people aren't seriously punished for not keeping the commandment to set aside the Sabbath as a day of worship.

CHARLIE: Well, the key idea of Christianity would be even *more* irrational for me to endorse—recognize Jesus as the son of God and my savior. If the specific system were the Catholic Church, I'd be living under a system that gave highest authority to the Pope. As a member of the deliberative committee, there's no way I could rationally endorse and help bring about the creation of a system like this, which would seriously limit my freedoms for no compensating gain.

MATT: But suppose the deliberative committee did endorse a religious system—specifically Christianity? Would the Christian system really impose those beliefs on everyone? That doesn't seem very Christian to me!

BEN: I'm not sure myself what determining the rationality of endorsing a religious system would be like in terms of endorsing its beliefs. I think it's clearer if we focus on the specific requirements the religious system outlines regarding how to behave, not regarding what to believe. That brings us to rules like the Ten Commandments. And there I think Charlie is right. Where the Ten Commandments accord with the moral rules, then, of course, there's no conflict with the moral system—religion and morality alike prohibit killing. But where the religious rules and requirements differ from those of the moral system, it's pretty clear that an atheist like Charlie could not rationally accept them, for the reasons he's noted.

MATT: Maybe then the deliberators wouldn't be focusing specifically on Christianity. It could be another religion, or perhaps religion in general.

BEN: Right. Though I think the deliberative results will be the same in any case. Perhaps deliberators could imagine, instead of a specific religion, a committee or legislative body of leaders of various religions that would come together to articulate principles to live by and guidelines for rewards and punishments in the society as they envision it.

But if we're actually comparing religion with the moral system, these principles would still have to be distinctively religious—meaning that they would be said to issue from some higher, supernatural power and be intended to apply to all aspects of life, including intimate relationships and private behaviors, not just the public behaviors that secular laws cover. Also, they would invest the power to interpret and enforce these religious principles in a body of legislators, whereas the moral system, as an informal system, cannot include any formal body that could replace or revise the moral principles themselves, which are independent of any culture or institution.

I've noted that any society that embraces the moral system will include within it governmental legislative bodies that create the formal secular laws necessary to protect members of that society. But these are different from religious laws in their intent and in their restricted scope of application. Also, societies that best emulate the moral system are likely to have secular legislatures that are subject to democratic control, something that has not been characteristic of religious legislative bodies or authorities.

MATT: But suppose the religion in control of the society thought of the specifically religious rules not as required restrictions on behavior but as recommendations for how to behave?

CHARLIE: But that's not how religions present themselves. It's the Ten *Commandments*, not the Ten *Suggestions*!

MATT: I'll grant that this isn't the way religions usually present themselves, but suppose, just for the sake of argument, that a system did merely *encourage* belief and adherence to some specifically religious rules. What would the deliberative committee say about a non-coercive religious system?

BEN: What exactly do you mean by "non-coercive"?

MATT: Well, the religion would not punish anyone for disobeying the purely religious rules, as opposed to the moral rules, which would still function in the way they would under a moral system.

BEN: Would your idea be that this non-coercive religious system still gets to promote its religion in preference to others?

MATT: Hmm. What if I said no, it doesn't have any preferential status in the system relative to other religions?

BEN: Would religion in general, in the system you are imagining, have any preferential status compared to atheist and other non-religious belief systems?

MATT: I think I see where you're going with this. If I say that religion doesn't have any preferential status at all, then it's not really a religious system that we're talking about. If it otherwise follows the moral rules, it's just the moral system.

BEN: Exactly. In the moral system, adherents of various religions, as well as atheists and agnostics, have the freedom to promote their various viewpoints. But no one may impose their views or preferred behaviors on others against their will. The adherent of some religion cannot compel anyone to attend their worship services. But the atheist cannot prevent anyone from attending either. Of course, if some religious behavior or doctrine becomes coercive toward non-believers, or even coercive within the religion, the prima facie right to practice that religion stops with regard to that particular coercive practice.

MATT: I agree with what you say about compulsion or coercion. In fact, this discussion is making me appreciate, more than I had, that there really is some genius to a society that promotes freedom of religion rather than some state-mandated religion. Those of us who believe that religion is both true and enriching of every believer's life have all we can really ask for in an open society. We're guaranteed that the society is not trying to foist some opposing religion on us—or even some watered-down religion that doesn't capture what we think is most valuable about our relation to God. And I would be the last person to want someone to join my religion because they felt forced to.

SHARIFA: I agree with Matt. As a Muslim, I've argued against social forces in this country that impose undue hardships on Muslims, for example, through discrimination. But of course I wouldn't want to go in the opposite direction, where Islam would be imposed on everyone else. Regrettably, there are contemporary Muslim societies that do that. They discriminate against non-Muslims or punish those who don't follow their own, sometimes really distorted picture of what Islam is all about, what it asks, and what it demands of believers. But such societies are going against the Koran, which says, "There is no compulsion in religion."

We've seen by now that there are two parts to this deliberative committee puzzle. Some non-moral system is put forward, and we find that it would be irrational for those who don't share a belief in that system—relativism, ethical egoism, or whatever it may be—to publicly endorse a society organized in accordance with that system. And we all agree by now, I think, that this applies to a religious system when, for example, the religion imposes obligations on believers that could not be rationally accepted by nonbelievers.

But in order for the deliberative committee idea to work, the other part of the puzzle has to come out right. In terms of what we've examined so far, we've seen that, except for a few possible and unusual cases, those like the ethical egoist who initially favor something in opposition to the moral system will not find it irrational to publicly endorse the moral system. Will the results be similar in the case of religion? Or might there be some religious believers who would find it irrational to publicly endorse the moral system? And if so, how badly does that harm the deliberative outcome favoring the moral system?

BEN: Matt has emphasized how religion generally supports morality. Because of this support, it's pretty clear that the vast majority of religious believers would not find anything irrational about publicly endorsing morality. They would probably largely agree that they already do this anyway insofar as they make religious commitments that they understand as supporting the moral rules and ideals as we have described them, using Gert's terms.

Difficulties in individual cases will arise, though. We've noted that some religious teachings and practices can be positively immoral. And since believers are often told that these teachings issue from God and that nothing is more important than understanding and serving God's will, some might believe that it's God's will to follow what is in fact an immoral path. If one adds to that a belief that God will eternally punish anyone who does not follow his commands, then there looks to be a scenario by which some believers would find it irrational to publicly endorse the moral system.

MATT: How so?

BEN: Suppose this sort of religious person came to believe—influenced by very fundamentalist, fear-mongering teachers—both that all infidels are evil and should be killed and that God has personally charged him with the duty to kill unbelievers, on pain of eternal punishment for the believer if he fails to carry out this duty. The wrathful God he believes in would not tolerate public endorsement of anything other than God's law. It looks like it would be irrational for such a believer to publicly endorse the moral system. He presumably would not find any compensating gain in going against God's will, since there's not much that could compensate for eternal suffering in hell.

MATT: But his belief is false. God would never act in these sorts of ways.

BEN: When we were discussing the racist, we could say that his racist beliefs were false, because there is plenty of empirical evidence against them. But even in that case, we had to allow the racist to bring those falsehoods into the deliberative committee. So we can't exclude false religious beliefs either. And these aren't beliefs that can be empirically confirmed or disconfirmed. Some, perhaps most, of those with these extreme beliefs about a wrathful God might be persuadable by other sorts of arguments and considerations. It might be that they would be persuaded, or ought to be persuaded, by the incoherence of trying to match this picture of such a wrathful and hateful God with the picture that is also typically presented in most religions of God as loving, just, and merciful.

But if a particular religion or sect *doesn't* present that contrary, loving, picture of God's nature and only tells its adherents of a wrathful and vengeance-seeking God, then there could in principle be some who on religious grounds would find it irrational to endorse morality.

SHARIFA: What does that mean then for the idea of justifying morality?

BEN: In practical terms, I think it does very little harm to that project. Professor Ishida wants to show that almost every person put on her deliberative committee would be rationally required to publicly endorse the moral system and would also find good arguments for behaving morally, provided the committee as a whole did in fact publicly endorse morality. She doesn't demand unanimous endorsement, so the existence of a few possible exceptions doesn't undermine the results she is hoping for.

Consider the picture of this particular believer—really a religious fanatic—who might find it irrational to endorse morality. It requires such an extreme and probably unlikely set of beliefs that it might describe only a tiny proportion of the population, if anyone at all. Religions that are entirely negative and fear provoking are unlikely to gain much traction. Virtually every religion will offer the believer *something* to counter the idea that his God is so full of hatred, so helpless to kill infidels himself, so demanding of murder as a test of faith, and so lacking in any sense of mercy or love toward those who are devoted to him that the believer himself must undertake to kill infidels on pain of eternal punishment.

Now suppose you consider even a slight modification of this extreme and implausible fanaticism. Remove the belief that God would impose eternal punishment on devoted followers in such a case. The overall set of beliefs might well be such that it's now rational for the believer to endorse the moral system. It would protect him from extremists of other religions. And, without the threat of eternal punishment, he may have no compelling reason to refuse to endorse morality.

Once you get beyond these sorts of extreme religious beliefs, I don't think there will be any doubt that the vast majority of religious believers not only would rationally endorse the moral system in the deliberative committee setting but would also find compelling reasons to strive to act morally in the conduct of their lives. They may think of morality as the way God wants them to act. They would very likely see the moral rules as compatible with the rest of their religious beliefs, even if they also believe that there's more to religion than following the moral rules and trying to practice the moral ideals.

SHARIFA: What about some of my own beliefs and preferences—very significant to me—that stem, at least in part, from my religion? Would this be like Christine's preference for vegetarianism—which we agreed was not something she could use to declare it irrational for her to endorse the moral system? Or, because it would be part of my religious orientation, would it be different, so that perhaps it *would* be irrational for me to endorse morality?

BEN: What do you have in mind in terms of those beliefs and preferences?

SHARIFA: Well, I don't like some of the ways that people behave in this society. No, it's more than dislike. I think it's wrong—morally wrong. I wear a hijab and dress conservatively because it's my tradition. And honestly, I find the way a lot of women dress in this culture really inappropriate. It seems so sexualized. I actually feel more free, more like I'm judged on the basis of my abilities and who I am, less on the shape of my body, when I dress this way. On the face of it, this seems different from the vegetarian case, because the dispute there concerns beings that aren't moral agents. But of course I, and other people with my perspective, are very much moral agents!

CHARLIE: I respect your right to dress the way you do, but maybe this is one of those examples of an unbridgeable ethical difference. Your culture says it's wrong for women to dress in revealing clothing, but most Americans don't think it's wrong.

SHARIFA: I understand what you mean when you talk about my culture, but remember that I was born and raised in this country. I'm just as American as you are.

CHARLIE: But you're critical of how a lot of women dress in our society. Aren't you making that moral evaluation from the perspective of Muslim culture?

SHARIFA: Yes, I suppose so. I know, as Al-Ghazali says, that I have the beliefs I do because of the culture I grew up in. But I'm not a relativist. I think there are reasons in support of my beliefs. I think Muslim culture is right about this. Even if I initially adopted these and other cultural practices because they're what my parents and my community presented me with, I've thought about them, and I've made them my own choices.

BEN: But what you're not going to get is universal acceptance of that dress code for women. Many members of the deliberative committee will find it irrational to accept a society in which women are required to dress in the ways you would like.

SHARIFA: I understand that. And I do think it would be wrong to impose that kind of dress code on a society as diverse as America is. But it's also not as simple as leaving it at that. I would love to see an American culture as a whole that did not have as much focus on sexuality, where pornography wasn't so widespread and accepted, where you wouldn't get assaulted by suggestive ads—on billboards, on TV, and on the internet, everywhere really—that seem to go further and further each year in order to get more attention for the product they want to sell. It's degrading and disgusting. Even though all this must feel normal and OK to a lot of people, that doesn't mean it really is OK. It's clear from our discussion of relativism that we can't say a practice or set of practices is morally acceptable just because it's widely accepted within a culture.

CHRISTINE: I see what you mean, Sharifa, bringing up the comparison with my favoring moral vegetarianism. If this case is like that one, then it would not be irrational for you to publicly endorse the moral system, even if you would prefer a system that didn't accept what you see as inappropriately sexualized behavior. You would be free to advocate for your preferred way of life within a society governed by the moral system, but you wouldn't be free to impose it on everyone else. Is that the way Sharifa's case would be analyzed, Ben?

BEN: I believe so. Sharifa is not saying that people should be forced against their will to dress a certain way. Charlie accepts Sharifa's right to dress as she does. Also, Sharifa talks about some practices as degrading or disgusting. But such feelings can't be connected up with morality as readily as many people assume. That something is perceived as degrading or disgusting matters morally only to the extent that someone is harmed by the practice.

Cultures have a lot of variation in what they count as disgusting or not disgusting. For example, in the sky burials of Tibet, when a person dies, the body is taken to a mountain top and flayed—cut into pieces—and left for the vultures to pick the flesh off the bones. To many Americans, that sounds disgusting, disrespectful, and degrading. But Tibetans treat the practice with great reverence and feel that it accords great respect to the deceased. To them, our common practice of burial in the ground may feel degrading. After all, why are worms better than vultures? Neither practice is in itself immoral. No one is harmed. The deceased can't be harmed because they're already dead. The feelings of the living aren't hurt because in each culture their own burial practice feels respectful and proper.

CHRISTINE: What if someone deliberately acts in a way that another finds deeply offensive? Say they bury a deceased Tibetan in the ground, knowing that this will be a degrading and disrespectful treatment in the eyes of the family of the deceased.

BEN: If they did this deliberately to hurt members of the family, then it's immoral, because it violates the rule against causing pain to others. If they thought they were being respectful and had no idea about the Tibetan cultural attitude, then they acted out of ignorance and are not blameworthy.

The analysis of disgust about burial practices can be applied also to feelings of disgust toward sexual practices. If no one is harmed, it's not a moral issue, even though some may feel disgusted by it. On the other hand, perhaps some of the things Sharifa is concerned about do lead to harm. Perhaps pornography does lead to more disrespect for and violence toward women. If so, then it is a moral question because of the harm it causes to women.

CHARLIE: Aren't you in effect saying that homosexuality is morally OK? A lot of people feel disgusted by it, but if it's between consenting adults it doesn't seem that it harms anyone.

BEN: That's right. It's hard to see how the moral system could declare consenting adult homosexuality as a moral wrong. Many people are disgusted by the idea of it, but the act itself does not seem to be harmful in the case of adults who are respectful of and care about each other. Laws or social behaviors that punish consenting homosexual behavior, or that deny gay people rights and benefits accorded to others simply on the grounds of their being gay, illegitimately challenge their status as fully autonomous moral agents. In this way, the moral assessment of homophobia mirrors our analysis of racism. You can't deny someone the full protection of the moral rules simply because of their sexual orientation, any more than you can legitimately do so on account of race.

MATT: When I was in Catholic school the nuns said homosexuality was unnatural.

BEN: Did you ask them what "unnatural" means? We have a lot of things that seem morally OK, or even quite good, that aren't part of nature independent of humans. Consider newly invented medicines and vaccines or medical technologies designed to extend healthy lives beyond their "natural" span.

Some people claim that, in homosexuality, the genitals are used in ways that don't contribute to the purpose of reproduction and that this is what makes it wrong. But that would seem to turn contraception and sex after menopause into immoral acts too. The general idea that it's wrong to put a body part to some use not intended by nature seems to me quite misguided. Assuming that one can talk about nature's intentions or purposes (which is a little odd since we don't think of nature as a person with intentions), presumably nature intended our digestive system to be for purposes of nutrition. It processes food so we can stay alive. But we eat stuff all the time that has no nutritional value whatsoever. Jelly beans are never going to make a significant contribution to one's health and nutrition! We'll eat a hot fudge sundae, topped with whipped cream and a cherry, because it tastes good. It's hard to see what's morally wrong with an occasional treat like that.

CHRISTINE: Lots of us feel guilty when we eat that sundae!

BEN: Sure. But that's usually because of personal goals people have for themselves, like wanting to lose weight. That *can* be a moral issue if one's diet is so unhealthy that one is substantially risking serious diseases or a shortened life. And issues of failure at self-control, as when one just can't resist that second helping of dessert, can have other moral implications. But my point is just that there can be, and actually are, plenty of cases where it's perfectly acceptable morally to have a scrumptious dessert treat. If it can be OK to use our body parts related to eating to do things that have no nutritive value, it's hard to see why it would always have to be morally wrong to use body parts related to reproduction to do things that have no reproductive value.

MATT: I have to say that I don't believe, anymore, what I was brought up to believe about homosexuality. It's one case where I think Catholic teaching is wrong. I don't think homosexuality is a choice any more than my own heterosexuality is a choice. I used to believe homosexuality was a sin. To me, it really did just seem so unnatural—so much against what the obvious point of sexuality seemed to be. But what Ben says about this helps provide some reasons in support of what I've come to believe anyway, more or less on my own. I thought I was sensitive to what it would be like for people who find themselves attracted to members of their own sex. I would say things like, "Criticize the sin and not the sinner." But that still meant criticizing people's actions as sinful when they give in to homosexual impulses that, I'm sure, are just as strong as my heterosexual impulses. I thought about how hard it would be for me if my religion said that it was heterosexuality that was the sin and that I had to either have relations only with other men or be celibate.

For a while, I accepted what my priest once said in trying to explain about how unfair this seemed. He said that God tested different people in different ways, that if one person was tested by sexual temptation to act in sinful ways while heterosexuals were not tempted in that way, well, each heterosexual person has his own trials. We don't always even know what that trial is. I guess with homosexuality, at least, it was supposed to be clear that this was God's test for you.

But I don't find my priest's explanation plausible anymore. I genuinely don't know whether God does indeed create challenges for each person. I don't know the mind of God. But in my own life and the lives of a lot of people I know, I don't see anything like the challenge of constant sexual temptation to sin, where my whole sexual identity is directed toward acts that are supposedly morally forbidden. It seems unfair to make some people have to live their lives under that kind of burden, when others like me don't.

SHARIFA: I've been like Matt was, thinking homosexuality obviously wrong, partly because it seems so unnatural. But what Matt says is pretty compelling. Most Muslims think it's wrong. But others of my faith think this judgment is unfair and have supported gay rights.

Most of the references to homosexuality in the Koran simply retell or comment on the story of Lot from the Bible. If Matt can see the message of love and moral acceptance here, so can I.

CHRISTINE: But still, there are a lot of people who believe it's a sin. What about them?

BEN: It remains to be seen how many of them would still believe it if they thought open-mindedly about it and listened attentively to the arguments, especially if they encountered a gay person in the deliberative context. In order for endorsement of the moral system to be irrational, it has to create significant harms to the potential endorser given her values. But a sense of disgust at what other people might be doing behind closed doors doesn't seem like it would typically create a sufficient amount of harm to the person who dislikes the thought of such activities.

SHARIFA: I'd like to get back to my initial concern about how people dress in this culture. I'm not against sexuality, but I believe it should be a private expression of love between two people. I really don't think it's right to have it be so openly and publicly expressed. It emphasizes the wrong things in terms of what makes for a good, loving, and long-term relationship, and it tempts those already in those relationships to stray. You said that it would be irrational for others to agree to a society in which everyone is forced to dress in the more modest manner I prefer. I understand that. And again I'm not saying that anyone should be forced to dress in this way. But doesn't it work the other way too? Wouldn't it be irrational for those like myself to endorse a society in which others dress in a way that we find to be so oversexualized? How people dress in public is not a behind-closed-doors matter.

CHARLIE: A society that forced women to dress a certain way would seriously restrict their freedom. That's quite different from a society in which people are free to dress in ways that others find offensive. It may be unpleasant to see things you don't like when you're in public, but it's not really the same as you being forced to do something against your will. The world is full of stupid commercials, ugly billboards, and annoying ads on the internet. They're pretty much unavoidable. But these are annoyances rather than limitations on your own freedom or on who you are and how you choose to express yourself.

SHARIFA: It's more than just stupid commercials. Maybe it's not a serious limitation on me, but if I have a daughter, I don't want her being exposed to this. It's pressure—pressure on her to be a certain way that I would be very troubled to see her become.

BEN: Charlie's right that there are differences here. I think the deliberative process itself will show that it's unrealistic for anyone to think that they can demand to live in a society where they are guaranteed not to be exposed, at least in some minor ways and perhaps occasionally in more serious ways, to things they feel are upsetting or disgusting. Perhaps some society could be structured that way—a society that enforces significant fines or imprisonment for a lewd gesture would definitely reduce the number of lewd gestures on the street. But surely many members of the deliberative committee would find it irrational to accept such a limitation on their freedom. Even if a lewd gesture is mean, to be human is to encounter meanness and other less salutary aspects of human nature. Most of us are thoughtless or rude at times and lose our tempers and do things we later regret. I couldn't rationally accept a society that imposed an overly severe punishment for my occasional failures along these lines, and I understand that others couldn't rationally accept a society that severely limited—with harsh punishments—the expression of things I happen to find lewd, rude, or disgusting.

SHARIFA: I see that it would be irrational for other deliberators such as you to endorse, as requirements for everyone, the practices and policies I favor. But the second component of the deliberative procedure is to address the question of whether *I* would find it irrational to endorse the moral system. *You* aren't the one who can determine how disgusted or upset I am by some of the ways people behave, act, or dress in society.

BEN: That's certainly true. But let me say a bit more about a point I mentioned a minute ago: Some weight has to be given to the idea that, in order for a proposed way of organizing society to be irrational for someone on the deliberative committee to endorse, the consequences of living in that society have to create a *significant* harm for the deliberator. The idea of how harmful something has to be to count as "significant" is of course vague. But as Aristotle said, morality can't have the precision of mathematics. Acknowledging this does mean that there are some cases where we just can't be sure whether the harm is significant enough, relative to the benefits, for it to be irrational for a particular individual to endorse morality. Sometimes it's just indeterminate.

SHARIFA: Well, then, maybe my case is indeterminate like that. Or maybe it really is irrational for me, given my values, to endorse the moral system. But this isn't something it's up to you to decide.

BEN: That's right, of course, because it does depend on your own values. But maybe as you talk more about what you really value we can think together about whether it's clear that endorsing morality is rational for you, or clearly irrational, or just indeterminate.

SHARIFA: So am I seriously harmed by what seems to me an inappropriate emphasis on sexuality in our culture? I'm thinking out loud here—it's interesting how this conversation itself is helping me clarify what I really believe and how I would balance the different things I value.

My first thought is that I believe this overemphasis on sexuality is harmful to women. Because of how I dress, I can avoid it. But there's all this harassment that goes on in our culture, so that sometimes it's impossible for women to walk down the street without being harassed. Even though I'm not a target, what if I have a daughter who wants to dress the way her peers do? I would worry about her being harassed.

BEN: But to the extent that there are such harms, the moral system offers protection against them. Such harassment is a deprivation of women's freedom. Unwanted attention also causes emotional pain and can negatively affect a young woman's development. So in a society under the moral system, people would take steps to keep women—including any daughter you might have—from being deprived of freedom or caused pain in these ways. Again, no human society is going to be perfect on this or any other moral score, but it's clear that different existing societies vary greatly in such matters as how women are treated when they walk down a street or otherwise are in public. In a society under the moral system, harassment will be strongly looked down upon and discouraged by informal or, in more serious cases, formal—meaning legal—punishments.

So the question to focus on here is your own level of discomfort or revulsion at what you see in public, not at the thought of or fear of being harassed, since those considerations would support endorsement of the moral system. Is that revulsion or disgust strong enough that you feel that the benefits of endorsing the moral system are outweighed by the harm to yourself caused by such feelings?

SHARIFA: I guess I'd have to say no, my unhappiness about it is not *that* strong, especially when I consider the protections afforded by the moral system. It's just hard to endorse a society that allows such behaviors and attitudes.

BEN: Oh, but on that point, do keep in mind that, as a deliberator, you are *not* endorsing a society with the specific attitudes toward dress or public expression of sexuality that our society happens to have. You are only making a general endorsement of the moral system. And that may well turn out to *support* your more specific views when those issues are more carefully examined. Though that examination is outside the purview of the more general task of Professor Ishida's deliberative committee, I could imagine it turning out that, in a society that takes morality seriously, people might come to understand that certain ways of presenting oneself are harmful enough that they should be at least informally discouraged. Maybe too much emphasis on women's bodies, such as does seem to be so prevalent now, will be shown to contribute to self-esteem issues among women and to health problems like anorexia. Of course, some of these are empirical questions rather than questions of morality proper. But under the moral system a society will be concerned to identify sources of harm and take seriously the support of empirical research toward that end.

CHARLIE: But I can't see a moral society denying women the freedom to dress in revealing clothing if that's what they want to do.

BEN: Maybe it could be analogous to what we discovered about cigarette smoking and its health issues. We've never made smoking illegal. People still have the freedom to smoke. But social attitudes toward it have changed, and usage has dropped significantly. Similarly, our behaviors and attitudes about practices related to environmental conservation, like recycling, have changed significantly as we've become more aware of global warming and other environmental effects of our patterns of consumption and energy use. These are examples of significant changes in social behavior motivated by ethical concerns as we have acquired more empirical information about the harmfulness of certain practices—examples in which the new practices have to a large extent been voluntarily followed.

CHRISTINE: There's also an interesting question here of whether women really *want* to dress in these ways. Or is there some subtle pressure on them to dress in the ways men want, so that maybe, in a less sexist system, women would not feel external pressure to dress a certain way? If so and if society were sensitive to this, women might then have more personal freedom to dress in a more self-expressive way, not necessarily in a seductive way.

I do see similarities between Sharifa's concerns about dress codes and mine about vegetarianism, even though they are different regarding whether the concerns are directed toward moral agents or toward animals that are not moral agents. The deliberators are deciding broadly on endorsing the moral system versus ethical egoism, a theocracy, or some other governing system. In endorsing the moral system, they aren't deciding that it's OK to kill animals for food, and they aren't deciding that it's OK for women to dress as they do in our culture. But the moral system allows for the most open discussion of our more specific views and values, and we can hope that those further discussions might go our way.

SHARIFA: Right. That point, together with Ben's point that I would not be endorsing a way of dressing that I don't approve of in endorsing the moral system, makes it pretty clear to me that it wouldn't be irrational for me, given my values, to endorse the moral system. It gives me everything I could want that is consistent with not imposing on others practices that would be irrational for them to accept.

So yes, I'm on board in terms of endorsing the moral system. But I'd just want to add that while I agree that some Islamic practices, like the requirement to pray five times a day, would not be rational for others to endorse, many of my faith's ideas and values are, I believe. I'm thinking of our teachings that urge us to alleviate suffering, to protect the weak and be generous to the poor, to act with compassion and kindness, and to come together as a community in support of these values. These *would* be specifically endorsed by the deliberative committee as rules that ought to be part of any society they could rationally accept.

MATT: Those are teachings that Christians take to be part of Jesus' message too.

BEN: But notice that we're back, again, to *moral* guidelines, as opposed to specifically religious and theological claims. This suggests, first, that one of the historically and culturally significant functions of religion has been to encode the message of morality—that we ought to care about others, reduce and restrict harmful practices, and encourage beneficial and helpful practices. And second, it suggests that this moral understanding is universal, even if it's sometimes imperfectly understood and sometimes confused with strictly religious practices based on metaphysical and theological beliefs that, whatever their truth, go beyond morality proper.

MATT: Sharifa, I have to ask you about one difference between Catholicism and Islam that I've wondered about. In Islam, isn't there a call for some kind of absolute humility or submission—an unquestioning devotion to God and the will of God? Can that be consistent with making your own ethical choices in life?

SHARIFA: I don't know that there's such a strong difference between them. Remember, in the comparative religion class, we discussed the Christian saying "Not my will, but thine be done." In any case, I do believe in humility and submission to the will of Allah. But believing in that can't be inconsistent with the freedom that Allah surely wanted me to have. I sometimes do argue with my parents about this. "Sharifa, be more humble," they'll say. But what is humility? "Oh, Sharifa!" they say when I ask that.

CHRISTINE: Well, when you're here with other philosophy students, we won't say that. It's a good question.

SHARIFA: I understand humility as the feeling that I carry with me all the time because of my knowing that Allah created this amazing world. In his wisdom and compassion he created everything—you, me, everything. I don't think there is any other good explanation for how all this came to be. One can only bow down in awe and in grateful submission in recognition of this. Sometimes I feel bad for atheists because they can't really have this experience.

CHARLIE [*in his best Eeyore imitation*]: Oh, don't worry about me. I'll probably manage somehow or other.

CHRISTINE: I don't know, Charlie. The world looks very different depending on whether or not you believe in God. It may really be that there's some appreciation of it that's closed to you as an atheist.

CHARLIE [*himself again*]: Well, sure, I'll accept that. But I'm not going to become a believer just so I can experience the world a certain way. And actually, it's kind of amazing in its own different way to believe, as I do, that this world came about on its own, without some creative intelligence.

CHRISTINE: But Sharifa, how does this humility work in your everyday life? You're a pretty spirited girl. Is that really consistent with submitting to the will of Allah?

SHARIFA: Oh, absolutely it is. Allah created me with all my curiosity and, I guess, energy. He created a joyful world that's a pleasure to be in and explore. He created us with our minds and our questions—think about how children delight in exploring their new world. Allah would not have given me my will and spirit and my capacity to reason and try to work things out for myself—and he wouldn't have given others these same qualities—if he didn't take pleasure in us and our use of his gifts.

At the same time, the call to submission reminds us that we can and do misuse his gifts and that we don't have all the answers. We are fallible and our own temptations lead us to misuse the will and freedom Allah granted us. When I'm confused or feel tempted to go in the wrong direction, my prayers and submission to his love and wisdom provide me the guidance I need. Then it's up to me to do my best to follow it!

CHARLIE: But how do you know when to make your own decisions and when to ask for help?

SHARIFA: I'm sure I don't get it right sometimes—and then I rely on Allah's mercy. Without a sense of submission, the enjoyment of the power of our own will can carry us too far into the morally bad or even the evil. I do overstep sometimes, and prayer and humility call me back to where I need to be. I couldn't manage that without Allah's guiding spirit. But I also love the freedom he has granted me to be who I am and to use my individuality to celebrate Allah and this world he has created.

MATT: That sounds exactly right to me. With God, or Allah, we're given assurance that there's help when we stray. Sharifa's just right that God would not have given us the free will he endowed us with if he didn't want us to use that freedom to express ourselves and to test ourselves and learn to confront the difficult choices that life inevitably presents. He didn't want puppets!

SHARIFA: Of course, I think Matt and I both understand, after this discussion, why we couldn't impose either Christian or Muslim religious practices, or religion in general, on others. Like you, Matt, I wouldn't want to. Others in any case couldn't rationally accept a society governed by our preferred theologies. But the moral system gives us the freedom to make our case to others, without having some opposing theology—or atheology for that matter—being imposed on us.

MATT: Charlie, it's not that I doubt your sincerity at all, but I'm curious how you think this conversation, the readings, and the class have changed you. You came into it supporting a pretty individualistic and, in fact, rather self-centered approach. And now you say you would comply with the moral system. Is it really like you've had a conversion experience? Have you seen the light—the moral light, in this case?

CHARLIE: You know, it isn't so much that I've really changed to something the complete opposite of what I believed before. It's more that the professor, the course, and especially our discussions have forced me to think more clearly. I think my views were just sort of a muddle. And I was a little worried about thinking about it too much. I wanted to do what I wanted to do! I knew that people could accuse me of being selfish, and it occurred to me that I could respond to that with the idea that we should all be equally selfish. I guess what I've come to understand is that the implications of that idea don't work out so well. To me now, it looks like that was just lazy thinking—a rationalization.

CHRISTINE: I'm still not satisfied, though. I *am* convinced by our earlier discussion that moral relativism isn't viable. I see now that my strongest motivations for thinking relativism true—my valuing of tolerance and my hatred of elitism—are really values that are *part of* the moral system and that relativism just doesn't work on its own terms. So I'm trying to root for the moral system now. And Professor Ishida's deliberative committee thought experiment is ingenious, but it's disappointing in some ways. You have to keep some people off the deliberative committee in order to get unanimous agreement—specifically, the religious extremist who thinks he'll be eternally punished for not killing infidels, the sociopath, and perhaps the egocentric strongman and some racists.

And the thought experiment acknowledges that some of those who do publicly endorse the moral system won't find a compelling argument to personally comply with it once they are living under the moral system. Of course, we've seen that there will be other cases, like Charlie's, where someone who enters the deliberative process with a fairly selfish attitude *will* find good arguments to personally abide by the moral system. But it seems like it's not really a successful justification of morality until we have an account that offers a compelling argument to *everyone* about why they ought to follow the moral system. Professor Ishida's account isn't everything a complete defense of morality could be. I wonder if we can't do better.

BEN: You may be right that there's something better we could reach for. But let's not underestimate what we do seem to have accomplished here: Each of you comes from a different background, and when we started these discussions you each had different critical takes on the idea of morality as a universal system to be preferred to all other systems for governing behavior. While Matt and Sharifa have supported universal morality from the start, I think they appreciate now that morality is not universal and objective because it's religious—that in fact it's independent of religion and religious systems—and that a secularist can embrace specifically moral values and principles just as fully as a religious believer can.

If each one of you on reflection now agrees that the arguments for you to publicly endorse and personally comply with the moral system are superior to any of the other options, including any religious system that would require the entire society to follow the rules and principles of that religion, then that goes a long way toward a quite important goal. It shows that, even with their different starting points in society and different religious and ideological beliefs, many ordinary people—perhaps most—will find that the best arguments are strongly in favor of their adopting the moral system in both word and deed. That's an achievement.

Now, *can* we go further and find the sort of master argument for complying with the moral system that Christine is hoping for? Professor Ishida is skeptical, but I do wonder if she's too pessimistic about that. Philosophy in general, and this problem in particular, are matters of open, ongoing inquiry. Keep thinking about it. Maybe you'll figure out a new approach that further extends and deepens our understanding of morality and strengthens the arguments that justify it.

# Ben's Conversation with Professor Ishida

*At the end of the semester. In Yuko Ishida's office.*

ISHIDA: Well, Ben, nice work. Students have been telling me about those long discussion sessions you've been having outside of class. And they've had great things to say about you. A supererogatory job on your part, I'd say.

BEN: Thanks, Yuko. But it didn't feel all that supererogatory. I'm finding that the best way to learn philosophy is to teach it. I've gotten at least as much out of our conversations as they have.

ISHIDA: So, philosophical dialogue being what it is, that probably means that you have a lot of questions that their own questions and comments raised for you.

BEN: Absolutely! Where do I start? One thing I've been thinking about is this: These students are really great. They're engaged and interested in questions about morality. If they weren't already disposed to take morality pretty seriously, they probably wouldn't have taken this course in the first place, and they certainly wouldn't have kept me from working on my dissertation proposal with all our long conversations—sorry about that, by the way.

ISHIDA: Well, as you said, you learn by teaching, so I say you can consider your conversations with them as a quite useful way of thinking about your dissertation.

BEN: Ah, that's very generous of you. But I promise I'll have a proposal to you soon now that the semester is over!

Anyway, one question I have is whether the conclusions they've come to can be extended to most other people. They've all come to agree that the moral system is something that they would publicly endorse and that they would do their best to comply with it in their personal lives. But a lot of people aren't going to be as initially well disposed as they are toward accepting such conclusions. Because you've allowed those on the deliberative committee to bring all their existing beliefs and values into their deliberations, I do wonder how much of the general population—beyond idealistic college students—would really fully embrace the moral system as a result of these deliberations.

ISHIDA: But it's not just college students, surely. Think of all the parents from all walks of life who really care about instilling moral values in their children and those who take the specifically moral aspects of their religious teachings to heart and try to live those values.

BEN: You're right, of course. It would be pretty elitist to think that the ranks of those who take morality seriously are largely drawn from the college educated. I didn't mean to suggest that. But there's another reality out there that you surely have to acknowledge. It's the world beyond the students in our class and beyond all the good parents and compassionate religious folk.

I think about all the people who seem to care little or nothing about morality, at least when it comes to certain parts of their lives. I think about all the hate and vitriol and plain evil large scale and small in the world. Just occurring to me at random: civil wars where civilians are killed indiscriminately and suspected enemies are routinely and summarily tortured then killed; husbands or wives who take pleasure in humiliating the spouse they used to love; kleptocrats who take billions of their nation's wealth for themselves, leaving their subjects impoverished and uneducated; backstabbing in the office; date rape; buildings that are badly constructed because of political corruption and that collapse on earthquake victims; parents who kill their toddlers because they're crying; students downloading papers from the internet and presenting them as their own work; societies that don't believe girls are worth educating; global warming caused by nations wealthy enough to avoid its worst consequences and creating the most harm in poor nations that didn't contribute to the problem; drug-enhanced athletes; governments intruding in people's lives where it's no business of theirs; terrorism; rich people buying the politicians who will make them richer; sex slavery; cyberbullying; the people who rob you with a gun as well as the ones who rob you with a fountain pen. Just to scratch the surface.

ISHIDA: It is quite a list, isn't it? But suppose we confront someone acting unethically and ask them about their behavior. Do they offer an excuse—ignorance, inebriation, dire poverty, abusive parents, mental illness, political oppression of their group, or whatever it may be? To offer an excuse is to implicitly *accept* the moral system. Excuses may well be exculpatory in some cases. But even when they are not, those who offer an excuse are accepting the legitimacy of the moral system, not criticizing it.

BEN: What if they don't offer excuses? I would expect that a lot of criminals who engage in deliberate and carefully planned crimes like hacking credit card data or robbing banks know perfectly well that others regard these actions as immoral, but they just don't care what anyone thinks.

ISHIDA: The question is: Do they have a good argument that challenges the moral system? I doubt that the typical criminal such as you're describing does. It will always be the case that some individuals will act immorally. What we're concerned about is whether their actions are supported by reasons that would pass the deliberative committee test. If they offer nothing more than "I don't care if you think it's immoral; I'm just going to do it!" it won't pass that test. The justification of morality is all about reasons. And if some crooks just do what they do without even offering excuses, they aren't attempting to justify anything.

BEN: You say that people's actual beliefs and values are in place in the deliberative committee. But then it seems that some criminals like this, placed on the deliberative committee, would simply refuse to agree to anything supporting morality or would even just refuse to go along with the whole deliberative process.

ISHIDA: Of course there will be people with such attitudes. But the deliberative exercise is hypothetical to this extent: Simple obstreperousness is not allowed. Deliberators must engage with other deliberators and put forward their actual beliefs and values.

BEN: What if their actual beliefs and values are just an incoherent mishmash of inconsistent and garbled ideas?

ISHIDA: Then the outcome may be indeterminate in the case of such deliberators. We'd have to treat these cases the way we treat cases in which it's irrational for someone to publicly endorse morality and acknowledge that agreement can be reached only if such individuals are not part of the deliberative process. And then we'd want to look at the set of individuals who would have to be excluded in order to look for patterns and to try to understand what this tells us about the limits of our justification project. But it's important to remember that the deliberative process itself will require deliberators to put forward their ideas in conversation with other deliberators, who will point out inconsistencies and unclarities in those ideas and beliefs. Deliberators with initially confused or unclear ideas will be required by the deliberative rules to do their best to sort these out.

BEN: Would there be some guarantee that they actually would sort things out?

ISHIDA: No. Some may just have conflicting sets of values that they can't resolve or place in some rank ordering. But the very act of having to think carefully about their beliefs and values would, I think, help many deliberators, especially those who hadn't given much thought to these matters before, see that they do have some priorities and reject some beliefs when an inconsistency is pointed out to them.

And this enforced reflectiveness will carry over not just to the question of public endorsement of morality but to the question of whether a deliberator should privately intend to comply with the moral system. Of course it's an empirical question, based on facts about individual psychologies, what proportion of people there are for whom the arguments overall favor resolving to act morally versus those for whom the arguments overall favor acting selfishly. Hume talked about the natural sympathies we have that make us care about others. Maybe it isn't *all* of us who have such sympathies, but I believe it's most of us. I don't think the fact that some of those who publicly endorse morality will be immune to arguments for complying with it in their personal lives should undermine the strength of the idea that many and perhaps most individuals will find that the strongest arguments, given their beliefs and values as honed and clarified in the deliberative process, will favor supporting the moral system in deed and not just in word.

BEN: What about religiously motivated crimes and terrorism, and all the violent religious rhetoric that can inspire it? Students like Sharifa and Matt see their religions in ways that are already quite compatible with the moral system. But a lot of believers seem to endorse doctrines contrary to the moral system, thinking that God endorses this.

ISHIDA: That's true enough. But, except for quite extreme beliefs, such as that God will eternally punish a believer for failing to undertake actions in God's name that violate morality, almost all religious believers in the deliberative context will be rationally required to publicly endorse the moral system, and most of them, I think, will find good arguments for personally complying with morality, given their religious beliefs.

BEN: But doesn't this require believers to ignore a lot of the violent language and apparent approval of violence in their religious texts and doctrines?

ISHIDA: Some critics of religion say that such language amounts to religious endorsement of violence and hatred, but I think these critics may be too unwilling to put such language in a larger context. Christians or Muslims like Matt and Sharifa don't need to be seen as ignoring or rejecting some claims made in the books they take as sacred manifestations of the word of God. Since these books contain clear and repeated statements emphasizing God as loving, compassionate, and merciful, it isn't unreasonable to understand all other statements in light of them.

BEN: But wouldn't such critics of religion say this is a skewed interpretation of the texts?

ISHIDA: Most believers would likely say that it's the interpretation that emphasizes violence that's skewed. I'm not sure how much an outsider like me can contribute to that discussion. I guess you'd have to call me a lapsed Buddhist. [*Laughs.*] If there can even be such a thing! Most Buddhists don't take a very hard line about doctrine, so there's a pretty wide range of belief that can still count as Buddhist.

In any case, I don't have any particular authority to say how a believer from some different religious background is supposed to weigh or emphasize the different doctrines, teachings, and textual claims within their religious tradition. The texts themselves seem to be open ended enough to allow reasonable interpretations with significantly different orientations. Even if some scholar studied the Bible, for example, in great depth and declared that, on the best account of the language used and claims made, God is to be understood primarily as a violence-advocating avenger, that isn't really to the point. The relevant concern for us is what ordinary religious believers bring to the deliberative table in determining, with other deliberators, the shape of their common society. On that score, the sociology of their religions—in particular, what the religious institutions teach their students—is more important in explaining actual beliefs than any scholarly textual analysis.

I read parts of the Bible because I wanted to see where some of the very religious students in my classes were coming from. I asked some of them what they made of the more sanguinary and violent passages. I was struck by the fact that most of them were as new to the passages as I was. These stories weren't at all emphasized, or they were completely ignored, in their Sunday Schools and sermons. Of course, there are exceptions. But there's also the danger of overemphasizing the exceptions because those are the cases that get prominent media coverage.

BEN: Is it really mostly a matter of sociology? Given the objective component of what makes an argument a good one for an individual, it could be that not as many believers as you would like are going to have good arguments for complying with the moral system, even if they're rationally required to publicly endorse it. Suppose that, as you suggest, the textual evidence for a vengeful and violent God or Allah isn't emphasized by most religious teachers. Still, isn't that evidence readily available to their students? This could be like the case of the man who suspects he has cancer but chooses not to acquire the evidence that would confirm this.

ISHIDA: The students may not even have the suspicion if they aren't directed to the passages.

BEN: But if the texts are readily available and the students are encouraged not only to read them but to treat them as the sacred and inviolable word of God, it seems that they should be reasonably expected to have this evidence of a violent Supreme Being.

ISHIDA: Even then, it's a matter of how they square such passages with the contrary presentations of God that they will also find in the texts. Most believers are not autodidacts. They are guided by their teachers. So it does remain primarily a question of what their teachers emphasize in the texts.

It's important to remember that much of what we know in general, or reasonably believe, comes from what authorities, teachers, and experts tell us, rather than from what we discover by our own investigations. This includes relying on religious authorities' interpretations of a religion, when the question concerns the meaning of that religion or its doctrines. Unless it's specifically required that the devout read and understand every word of the sacred text, it can be reasonable for a believer to base his understanding of his religion on what his priest, preacher, imam, rabbi, or guru teaches him. And that means, in my view, that a lot of believers will reasonably believe in a loving God or spirit, whatever some seemingly objective data mining of the religious text tells us.

Concerning those who do, in the name of religion, foment or carry out violent actions, I do wonder whether they are really motivated by a genuine belief in some supremely vengeful and unloving deity. This is another empirical question, but it could be that many such individuals are actually motivated primarily by the same factors that lead to serious crimes that aren't religiously motivated: greed (perhaps the desire for heavenly rewards rather than financial ones in some cases), personal hatreds and animosities, group allegiance, perceived slights to one's group or genuine political oppression, and so on. If that's right, then the assessment of deliberative outcomes in such cases would be more like those of the more typical, secular immoralists we've already discussed.

BEN: That sort of psychological motivation may explain some cases, and I do agree that most believers hold pacific interpretations of their religions. But I still wonder if the number of those who believe in a sacred justification for violence is all that marginal. As you note, it's an empirical question, and I don't think it has a clear-cut answer.

Another thing I've been curious about is the status of moral truths. What explains the objectivity of morality for you? Doesn't it have to be that this can only be explained by holding that moral truths must exist independently of humans and human societies? If mathematical truths are objective discoveries as opposed to subjective or intersubjective inventions, as seems to be required when we posit that intelligent civilizations from elsewhere in the galaxy would presumably discover the same truths of mathematics that we recognize, then doesn't this also support the idea that the moral system is an objective discovery as opposed to a human invention?

ISHIDA: That sounds very Platonistic to me. Do you really want to posit a realm of abstract truths independent of and detached from human existence—indeed independent of the physical universe we know and love?

BEN: We have to do it in the case of mathematics. So once we've posited that mathematical realm, we've already got the metaphysical room for abstract moral properties and principles, it seems to me. If the abstract mathematical principles or truths are there, we might as well invite in the abstract moral truths.

ISHIDA: That's very hospitable of you, Ben! But for one thing, not everyone agrees with you about the status of mathematical truths. Platonists don't hold sway. And more importantly, even if there is some room for mathematical truths as abstract realities and numbers as abstract objects, it doesn't follow that moral truths must be treated the same way.

BEN: I would say that for any civilizations with individuals who are, like us, mortal, vulnerable, and fallible, these same moral principles would have to apply. So morality is transhuman. Other civilizations would discover these same principles. It seems plausible to me to conclude that morality is objective and timeless in the strong sense that it would still exist even if humans had never evolved.

ISHIDA: That's pretty speculative, Ben. I'm inclined to keep to what I think we can have some reason to affirm. Philosophy is speculative enough as it is! And I think you'd have a hard time defending your Platonistic implication that these moral principles have some real status as abstract eternal verities, existing even if no intelligences at all existed in the universe. What we do know is that we humans have those properties you mention—mortality, vulnerability, and fallibility. This is the human condition. I don't really know about other possible civilizations elsewhere in the cosmos, how like or unlike us humans they might be, or what we would or should say about any differences between us and them. I think that the moral system as we know and understand it is something that emerges from our human condition.

BEN: Isn't there some danger of relativism if you go this route? It seems to make morality relative to what human beings do and think.

And if you accept that, then why not relativize morality to what different cultures do and think? You're back to cultural relativism!

ISHIDA: I don't accept that slippery slope. I think we can affirm morality as universal in a quite strong sense, based on what all humans who are moral agents manifestly do have in common—our ability to reason, our deliberative capacities, our cognitive fallibility, and our physical vulnerability. Any attempt to locate the *basis* of morality in specific social systems or cultural arrangements, where these vary across societies, would not be able to achieve such universality because of those variations. And we know that cultures can go astray morally, so cultural relativism is not seriously in play. The question is whether what we all do have in common can provide the basis for a universal morality. I think it can.

BEN: Suppose, though, that we become physically *in*vulnerable. There's actual talk of how maybe we will learn to download our brains onto computer chips. Maybe we can clone copies of our physical bodies and upload our memories and personalities to new physical brains placed in those bodies, allowing our sense of ourselves as the persons we've been, with our memories and personalities, to continue. Some people even say this could happen in this century. If we achieve that, it's a kind of immortality and invulnerability, isn't it?

ISHIDA: I'm doubtful about the prospects of this. But even if it happened, I think we're still vulnerable. As long as there's a required physical basis for being a person, as I believe there must be, then the center of consciousness, memories, and self-identity that constitutes an individual mind can cease to exist if and when that physical basis ceases or becomes corrupted. Besides, all this technology, even if it came to fruition, is not going to make us infallible.

BEN: Then where are you on the question of evolution and morality? You seem to have a pretty naturalistic take on things. You think we are essentially biological organisms who have evolved minds and consciousness, not immaterial souls. So would you also say that understanding human evolution holds the key to understanding human morality?

ISHIDA: You know, I'm sure, about evolutionary psychologists who say that there are evolutionary explanations for altruistic traits like caring for others, making sacrifices for the sake of others, and so on. These traits may help the group survive even at the expense of the individual. If some individuals sacrifice themselves, for example, engaging in dangerous but useful activities in which they expose themselves to predators or enemies, then the group or species itself has its survivability chances enhanced. This can be genetically driven, because a group typically consists of kin who share genetic material. So a lot of behavior that we think of as moral might have arisen from evolutionary selection pressures. At the same time, some *im*moral behavior might also be wired into our evolutionary heritage. They say a male lion will kill young cubs sired by another male then mate with their mother, enhancing his own genetic profile. Promiscuity can do the same. Evolutionary psychologists suggest that perhaps some of these less salutary behaviors also have an evolutionary explanation.

BEN: So what does that say about morality? Are our behaviors determined by some sort of evolutionary imperative? And if so, does that mean that morality is illegitimate—that it's just a meaningless ideology that we believe in because we think we're special—that we can't really face the fact that we are kin to gorillas and microbes?

ISHIDA: Well, what do you think, Ben?

BEN: I don't think these considerations undermine the legitimacy of morality. It's clear that we don't operate by instinct. It's good to know about the possible evolutionary explanations for some human impulses and emotions. That can help us understand better some of our behavioral tendencies, both good and bad. But we've also evolved the capacity to reason and to use reason to change our behavior, including learning to resist impulses to behave in certain ways. Maybe there's some genetic component to aggressive behavior, for example. But that doesn't mean a normal adult human can excuse himself after he kills his toddler stepson on the grounds that his genes made him do it or that, since lions do it, this justifies his doing it. Or do you see morality more under threat here?

ISHIDA: It's a complex story about which a lot more could be said. But I do agree with you. Reason gives us the capacity to deliberate, and that capacity makes us morally responsible for our actions, unless we are incapacitated by insanity or some other mental illness or cognitive impairment.

BEN: So you're not a biological determinist in the sense of believing that moral properties can be reduced to biological properties or that morality is determined in some fundamental way by genetics.

ISHIDA: No. I'm enough of a naturalist to believe that our capacity to reason is a capacity of our brains, which evolved as they did in part because being able to reason enhances our survival. But once we've got that capacity, we're not in thrall to instinct anymore. We become moral agents. We know we can hurt other people and that they don't want to be hurt by us. We can choose actions that avoid unnecessary harms or, when we fail to make those choices, we can and should be held responsible. I guess I don't make as much of it metaphysically as you do, but I do think we operate under a new system—the moral system rather than a purely biological one.

BEN: Do you think this capacity is unique to humans? Could some animals be moral agents?

ISHIDA: It's pretty clear that an earthworm or a chicken doesn't have that capacity. I doubt if chipmunks deliberate about the morally correct course of action or that an owl has any second thoughts after catching and eating that chipmunk.

BEN: But what about the great apes? Some primatologists who have observed chimpanzees and other primates in the wild have suggested that one might attribute morality to them and that different individuals can have good and bad moral characters.

ISHIDA: This is an interesting question. Is language a prerequisite for moral agency? There's a lot of empirical knowledge that we don't yet have about the capacities of these animals and that we need before we can be fully confident of the right answer.

On the general question of whether morality can be explained as something more than our biology, I think that the answer isn't just that our capacity to reason allows us to escape the bonds of evolutionary programming. That still doesn't tell us what reason will actually say about the value of morality compared to egoism, for example. On that matter, I think that one does need a philosophical justification of morality if we are to fully answer the question of what morality is and why we should act morally.

BEN: About your justification, though, I appreciate what it does accomplish, but I do wonder about its limitations. I think most philosophers who have looked for arguments justifying morality or for an answer to the question "Why should I be moral?" will be disappointed in your justification, since it doesn't offer a positive argument that will work for everyone. Certainly, your account does have practical value in that it does provide individual compelling arguments for endorsing and complying with morality in many cases. But most philosophers have looked for something more—a more general argument that clinches the case in justifying the moral system over its alternatives.

ISHIDA: I understand the dissatisfaction with the empirical and noncomprehensive elements of my deliberative thought experiment. If you can offer another route to the justification of morality, I'd love to see it. In my view, the idea that the very notion of rationality entails acting morally if you just work through the concept of rationality carefully enough is a nonstarter. It's been tried and found wanting.

And if that's so, then let's not neglect the virtues of the sort of justification of morality I've argued for. If philosophers hang everything on the quest for a rigorous argument showing a relation of logical entailment between rationality and morality and that argument fails, then where are we in relation to the skepticism shared by many philosophers, as well as a broader population of thoughtful individuals in contemporary culture, regarding the justification and status of morality? If, in a response to such skepticism, we can show that there are reasonable arguments—multiply sourced and variously structured given individuals' different worldviews—in favor of at least *those* individuals complying with the moral system, then we have everything wanted regarding an argument for being moral in the case of the particular individual in question.

That's not just a practical victory for morality in the case of that one person. I think my procedure can be used to defend a universal and objective morality even if it doesn't offer a resolution that supports morality in every case.

BEN: How so?

ISHIDA: It allows us to look for patterns in the cases where it's either irrational for a person to publicly endorse the moral system or he does not have a compelling reason to comply with it. I don't think that the fact that arguments to endorse or comply with morality occasionally don't succeed supports a skeptical stance about objective morality. And I think looking at such patterns can help explain this.

For example, the religious fanatic who believes God will punish him eternally if he fails to do something deeply immoral like kill infidels is in effect intimidated into his immorality. Given the fanatic's conception of God's demands upon him, he's not really making a genuine choice, any more than is the man who signs a contract because someone is pointing a gun at him. Instead of trying to oppose the fanatic's worldview by getting into a theological debate with him, we can see that the failure to endorse morality here is really a failure on account of an individual's lack of freedom.

That point can provide its own support, independently of any attempt to show a logical relation between rationality and morality, for the objectivity and universal scope of morality. We can say, in such a case, that the moral conclusion isn't reached because the fanatic doesn't have the freedom we take to be a prerequisite for moral responsibility. The moral system still applies to the fanatic, but morality does allow for exculpatory conditions. If anyone actually has such an extreme view as this, such an exculpation would seem to apply. But this would not necessarily get other religious extremists, with other belief sets, off the hook. This whole approach needs further exploration, but it suggests that there may be other ways to explain the failure to endorse or comply with the moral system in other types of cases.

BEN: That's an interesting avenue to explore. But do you think the idea of one master argument favoring morality, instead of these more individualized arguments, is a lost cause?

ISHIDA: Not at all. Again, I think it *is* a lost cause to hope for an a priori argument deducing morality from the concept of rationality. But there are plenty of other avenues, including some that, I'm sure, have never been fully worked out or even articulated yet, that might offer a more comprehensive justification of morality than mine does.

In fact, I think I'm seeing into your future, Ben. Here's your dissertation topic!

BEN: Yikes! I'm supposed to figure out a justification of morality that applies to everyone—a task that has eluded all the great moral philosophers to date? [*Laughs.*] Christine was asking about this possibility at the end of our discussions, and I rather airily suggested that maybe this was a problem she and the other students could work out someday. Now you're looking at me like *I'm* the one to do it?

ISHIDA: Your topic could be to do your best to figure it out and then report to the rest of us the results of your efforts. Maybe you'll be successful—in which case, great. But if not, that's great too, if you move the inquiry further along. You'll have understood more clearly what some of the obstacles are to such a global justification of morality or maybe even shown why it's impossible. In any case, whatever you find, you will help deepen our understanding of morality and the moral system.

BEN: But that might not be the positive conclusion philosophers would be looking for.

ISHIDA: Philosophers don't care so much what specific conclusion you end up with. We're more interested in what new arguments you find or how you extend the old arguments into a new area. Something new and interesting to think about.

BEN: You make it sound like it's just a game.

ISHIDA: It can look that way sometimes. But as I see it, one of our main goals as philosophers is to try to reach the truth, whatever it may be. In order to do that, we want to seek out the best arguments on all sides of a debate. What looks like game playing is really, I think, openness to all the arguments and doing one's best not to decide the case prior to having thought hard about all the possibilities. A good philosopher will follow the good arguments, wherever they may lead.

# Glossary

*A priori*: Known or knowable independently of sensory experience or empirical investigation; for example, mathematical statements and statements that are true by definition ("A bachelor is an unmarried man").

*Biological determinism*: The hypothesis that behavior, typically understood as including morally evaluable human behavior, is the product of a species' evolutionary history and an individual's genetic makeup to an extent significant enough to undermine traditional beliefs about individual free will or moral responsibility.

*Common morality*: The set of beliefs about morality alleged to be held in common by everyone. In Bernard Gert's account, it includes moral rules (for example, "Do not kill," "Keep your promises"), moral ideals such as acting kindly and helping those in need, and an understanding of general conditions under which a moral rule may be justifiably broken.

*Egoism vs. egotism*: An egotist is a self-centered person. Theories of egoism, by contrast, argue for views that emphasize the value of the self or that favor self-interest. An advocate of a theory of egoism is not necessarily an egotistical person. See also *ethical egoism*.

*Empirical*: Relating to the means of acquiring knowledge or evidence through our sensory experience of the world and through scientific investigation.

*Epistemology*: The branch of philosophy concerned with the nature of knowledge and evidence, with skeptical challenges to claims that knowledge is possible, and with the conditions required in order for our beliefs to be reasonable or justified.

*Ethical egoism*: The theory that an action is morally acceptable if and only if it is in the interests of the person undertaking that action. Often classed as a moral theory, ethical egoism is treated in this book as a theory that is critical of morality, because it lacks the other-regarding feature that is essential to the moral point of view.

*Ethics*: The philosophical study of morality. The term can also refer to a specific body of moral principles ("medical ethics," "Buddhist ethics"). "Ethical" and "moral" are treated as synonymous terms in this book.

*Haragei*: A Japanese conversational practice of speaking indirectly or noncommittally to avoid giving offense.

*Hijab*: Head scarf worn by some Muslim women.

*Kantian morality*: A moral theory focused on the agent's intent to do her duty, rather than on the consequences of her action. In Kant's system, all specific moral commands flow from a single fundamental principle—the categorical imperative. The emphasis in Kantian morality is on an action's universalizability (roughly, its being done for a reason that the agent performing the action could reasonably or consistently accept as a reason everyone could adopt) and on respect for other moral agents' intrinsic worth, entailing that a person may not treat another moral agent merely as a means to her own ends.

*Moral agent*: Someone capable of acting on the basis of reasoned deliberation, not just instinctually or blindly. Only moral agents can be held responsible for their actions.

*Moral system*: As used in this book, (1) a general description applying to any of a set of specific moral theories that include Kantianism, Utilitarianism, and the system of common morality as articulated by Bernard Gert; (2) the set of features that all these theories are said to have in common: They all articulate principles for regulating interpersonal behavior that are understood as universal and timeless, impartial, other-regarding, categorical (they judge certain types of actions to be acceptable, other types unacceptable), and having content that aims to encourage helpful behaviors and discourage harmful ones.

*Naturalism*: A metaphysical view that everything that exists is in some sense natural. Opposed to supernaturalism, which posits God or gods and other entities or forces beyond the physical but capable of interacting with it, for example, through miraculous intervention or ensoulment. Naturalism is associated with scientific realism, the view that science can, at least in principle, describe and explain everything that exists.

*Nihilism*: In general, the rejection of something that has traditionally been highly valued; for example, God, the possibility of genuine happiness, or the legitimacy of government. Moral nihilism rejects the view that there are any moral truths. It holds that belief in morality is merely a false ideology.

*Other-regarding*: An attitude that understands other moral agents as deserving of one's respect and consideration and, especially, as deserving not to be harmed without cause.

*Platonism*: The view associated with Plato that abstract objects have independent existence. Plato suggests that these objects, which he calls the Forms, are more truly real than the ordinary objects of everyday life. The Form of Circularity perfectly exemplifies what actually existing circles can only imperfectly represent. Contemporary Platonists defend the weaker claim that abstract objects, for example, the number 12, exist independently of all concrete existing things and cannot be explained or understood simply as features of human thought or language.

*Rational/irrational*: In Bernard Gert's use of the terms, adapted here, an action is irrational for a person to perform if it would significantly harm her interests without providing her with any compensating gains. A rational action is any action that is not irrational.

*Reasonable*: Said of beliefs, hypotheses, and theories that are adequately supported by evidence or by good arguments.

*Relativism*: Two varieties of moral relativism are discussed in this book. Subjective relativism is the view that an action is morally right if and only if the person performing the action believes it's right. More extensively discussed is cultural relativism, which holds that an action is morally right if and only if it is approved of in the culture in which it is performed. Another type of relativism, not discussed in the dialogue, is metaphysical relativism, which maintains that there are no objective truths; anything claimed true is only true from the perspective of a particular person, culture, or intellectual orientation.

*Supererogatory*: Above and beyond the call of duty.

*Utilitarianism*: A moral theory focused on the consequences of actions, promoting those actions that have the most socially beneficial consequences.

# Further Readings

Al-Ghazali, Muhammad. *Al-Ghazali's Path to Sufism and His Deliverance from Error*. Translated by R. J. McCarthy. Louisville, KY: Fons Vitae, 1999.

Baier, Kurt. *The Moral Point of View*. Ithaca, NY: Cornell University Press, 1958.

Gauthier, David. *Morals by Agreement*. New York: Oxford University Press, 1986.

Gert, Bernard. *Common Morality: Deciding What to Do*. New York: Oxford University Press, 2004.

Gert, Bernard. *Morality: Its Nature and Justification*. Rev. ed. New York: Oxford University Press, 2005.

Habermas, Jürgen. *Moral Consciousness and Communicative Action*. Translated by C. Lenhardt and S. W. Nicholsen. Cambridge: Massachusetts Institute of Technology Press, 1990.

Hills, Alison. *The Beloved Self: Morality and the Challenge from Egoism*. New York: Oxford University Press, 2010.

This book undertakes a project of the sort that Professor Ishida encourages Ben to work on.

Hobbes, Thomas. *Leviathan*. Edited by Edwin Curley. Indianapolis: Hackett, 1994.

Karam, Vanessa, Olivia Samad, and Ani Zonneveld, eds. *Progressive Muslim Identities: Personal Stories from the U.S. and Canada*. West Hollywood, CA: Oracle Releasing, 2011.

Nietzsche, Friedrich. *On the Genealogy of Morality*. Translated by Maudemarie Clark and Alan J. Swensen. Indianapolis: Hackett, 1998.

Parfit, Derek. "Nietzsche." In *On What Matters*, vol. 2, edited by Parfit and Samuel Scheffler, 570–606. New York: Oxford University Press, 2011.

Parfit argues that Nietzsche is not as antithetical to common morality as he is widely understood to be and that many of Nietzsche's most controversial claims about morality are based on false nonmoral assumptions, for example, about human psychology.

Rawls, John. *A Theory of Justice.* Rev ed. Cambridge, MA: Harvard University Press, 1999.

Sartre, Jean-Paul. *Existentialism Is a Humanism.* Translated by Carol Macomber. New Haven, CT: Yale University Press, 2007.

Triplett, Timm. "Justifying Morality, Part II: Beyond Justification as Clarification." *Journal of Value Inquiry* 45, no. 4 (2011): 403–17.

Yamamoto, Yutaka. "A Morality Based on Trust: Some Reflections on Japanese Morality." *Philosophy East and West* 40, no. 4 (1990): 451–69.

Ideas from this article are summarized by Sharifa in the "Exploring Morality across Cultures" section of the dialogue.